Blundering
Into
Disaster

ROBERT McNAMARA

Blundering Into Disaster

Surviving the First Century of the Nuclear Age

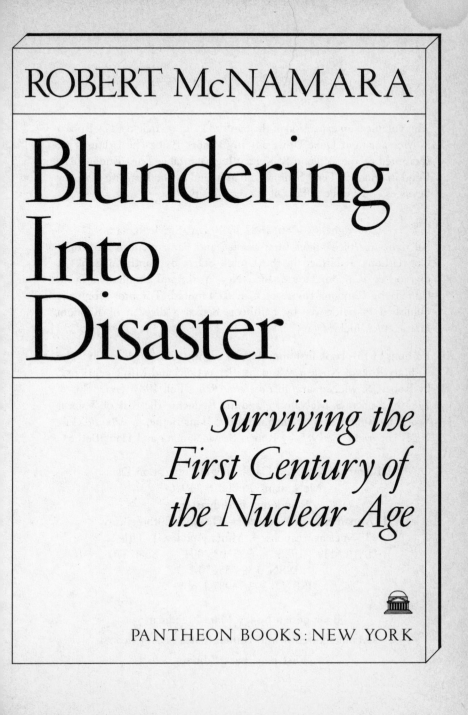

PANTHEON BOOKS : NEW YORK

This volume is an expansion of the Sanford Lectures delivered by Robert
S. McNamara at Duke University in October 1986. The Lectures are
sponsored by the William R. Kenan, Jr., Charitable Trust Endowment
Fund in honor of Terry Sanford and arranged by the Institute of Policy
Sciences and Public Affairs of the University.

Library of Congress Cataloging-in-Publication Data
McNamara, Robert S., 1916-
Blundering into disaster.
1. Armaments. 2. Arms race—History—20th century.
3. Nuclear weapons. 4. Military policy. I. Title.
UA10.M39   1986   355'.033'004   86-42870
ISBN 0-394-55850-2
ISBN 0-394-74987-1 pbk.

Book design by Joe Marc Freedman
Manufactured in the United States of America
First Paperback Edition

In memory of Margaret, one of God's loveliest creatures, who for forty years inspired me to pursue the values we shared.

And for Margy, Kathy, Craig, and the others of their generation who, together with their elders, must determine what risks are to be imposed on the world in the second half century of the nuclear age.

Contents

Foreword

On October 11, 1986, just as the first edition of this volume was rolling off the presses, President Reagan and General Secretary Gorbachev met in Reykjavik, Iceland. There they held the most far-reaching arms control talks since World War II. The manuscript had been finished and sent to the printer four months earlier, long before there was even a hint that a momentous summit meeting was soon to take place. However, the original text, in a very real sense, lays out the intellectual foundations for the Reykjavik discussions, outlines the elements of the arms control agreement that would have been in the interest of both parties, sheds light on why the negotiations failed, and points to the steps that now need to be taken to bring the parties back to the bargaining table.

The most important issue tentatively agreed on during the Reykjavik meeting was that there should be a "50 percent" cut in strategic offensive nuclear forces—from the roughly twelve thousand warheads held by each side today, to about six thousand. The reductions were to be phased in over a period of five years.

The tentative agreement on "first phase" reductions in strategic offensive forces was accompanied by an agreement on reductions in intermediate-range nuclear forces in Europe, and by discussions of further reductions in strategic forces over a ten-year period. There was even talk of the possibility of ultimately eliminating all nuclear weapons. There were hints as well that the negotiations would be expanded over time to include the the participation of the other nuclear powers, and to consider the steps to be taken to assure a better balance of Warsaw Pact and NATO conventional forces in the event that nuclear forces were reduced to near zero.

ix

But, in the end, the sticking point at Reykjavik centered on President Reagan's Strategic Defense Initiative.

The President insisted that for the next ten years the United States be permitted to carry out a broad program of research, development, and testing of antiballistic missile systems. At the end of that period, after all strategic offensive nuclear missiles on both sides had been destroyed, the United States would be permitted to deploy the SDI. Gorbachev countered by proposing that for ten years the SDI be limited to research "within the walls of the laboratory." Reagan said, in effect, "Why would Gorbachev object to development and deployment of defenses?" and Gorbachev said, "Why would Reagan wish to deploy defenses when there are no offenses?"

The President emphasized that, in his view, antiballistic missile defenses would be needed—even after the elimination of strategic offensive nuclear forces—in order to prevent cheating.

Gorbachev, however, believes that the United States is ahead in SDI technology today, and he fears that with unlimited testing and development it will forge even further ahead in the future. He foresees that at a time of its own choosing—perhaps six or seven years from now—the United States will unilaterally abrogate the ABM Treaty and thus place the Soviet Union in grave danger. And why would the USSR be in danger? Because the United States would have six thousand strategic offensive warheads, which it could pre-emptively launch against the Soviets, destroying a substantial percentage of their six thousand by such an attack, and be capable of destroying most of their remaining warheads as they attempted, in a retaliatory strike, to penetrate the U.S. defensive shield. In those circumstances the Soviets believe the United States would be able to subject them either to political blackmail or to military destruction.

Now I am convinced that this is not the President's objective. The Soviets are fearful of something the President does not intend. But from their point of view there is basis for concern. And the fact is that if the roles were reversed, and if they were proceeding as we are, we would be equally concerned.

Is there then a way out of this impasse? Can we reconcile the President's dream—his determination to probe the technological potential of missile defense systems—with Gorbachev's fear that we are moving toward a first-strike capability?

What kind of an agreement is now possible?

To begin with, the United States must accept the fact that there can be no restriction on strategic offensive nuclear arms that does not rest on a restriction of defensive forces, such as is now provided by the ABM Treaty. That is the foundation upon which the entire SALT process was originally based.

SALT was an American initiative. In November 1966 President Johnson and I first proposed to the Russians that we begin moving toward limits on strategic forces. We spent a long day at Glassboro, New Jersey, in 1967 trying to persuade Premier Aleksei Kosygin that development of strategic defenses on either side would fuel the arms competition and increase the danger of war, whereas constraining such defenses would make it possible for both sides to first limit and then reduce offensive arms. Five years later, in the SALT I accords, President Nixon finally got Soviet agreement on this very proposition.

So I repeat, first and foremost we must preserve the integrity of the ABM Treaty. Without it we will be unable even to begin the process of arms reduction.

But preserving the integrity of the ABM Treaty does not mean that the United States must agree to the Soviet demands that SDI research be carried out "within the walls of the laboratory." The United States can continue, as the President has proposed, to probe the technological potential of defensive systems. But the United States must not move into unrestricted development and testing of such hardware. That would be a clear violation of the treaty. And, as I have said, it would serve to fuel the Soviet fears that we mean to deploy the defensive systems, at a time of our own choosing, in clear violation of the treaty.

For both the present and future administrations, I cannot overemphasize the importance of recognizing the linkage between restrictions on strategic offensive nuclear forces and restrictions on defensive systems.

If it is accepted that the SDI program will be carried out in accordance with the terms of the ABM Treaty, as it has been traditionally interpreted, then the two parties can proceed to negotiate reductions in offensive forces similar to those proposed at Reykjavik for the "first phase." Elimination of intermediate- and short-range missile forces in Europe, and deep reductions, on the order of 50 percent, to a new limit of six thousand strategic warheads on each side, should be pursued. It would be particularly important that, within the total of six thousand, limits be established on particular weapons systems—e.g., highly accurate land- or sea-based systems—in such a way as to enhance what is known as "crisis stability."

The objective would be to reduce or eliminate each side's fear that the other is seeking to achieve a first-strike capability.

Reagan's and Gorbachev's intuitive reactions that we must change course, and their proposals for deep cuts in offensive nuclear forces, are correct. The debate surrounding these issues may well rage on for years, far beyond the term of Reagan's presidency. But to continue the escalation of the nuclear arms race would be totally irresponsible. We can and should seek to take a major step toward ending it by building on the foundations laid down at Reyjavik.

Washington, D.C.
April 30, 1987

Preface

During the seven years I served as Secretary of Defense, under Presidents Kennedy and Johnson, both U.S. and Soviet understanding of the political and military implications of the introduction of nuclear weapons was evolving slowly. In the following thirteen years, while president of the World Bank, I was unable to participate in the debate that developed over how best to strengthen our security in a nuclear world—discussions of test bans, nuclear freezes, new weapons programs, arms control agreements, etc. In the past five years I have done so through publication of a series of articles, often in association with others, in *Foreign Affairs* and the *Atlantic Monthly,* and through lectures before the Council on Foreign Relations and on university campuses.

As my own thinking has advanced, I have become more and more concerned that our nation—and indeed the world—needs a vision of the long-term objectives for nuclear force levels, military strategy, and arms control agreements that will minimize the risk that in this nuclear age, conflict between the great power blocs will lead to the destruction of our civilization. Such objectives, to be reached by the end of the century or in the years beyond, would guide, in the intervening years, our weapons development programs, our relations with our NATO allies, and our arms control negotiations with the Soviets.

In this small volume, which is an expansion of my Sanford Lectures to be given at Duke University, I shall put forward such a program.

Washington, D.C.
June 9, 1986

Blundering
Into
Disaster

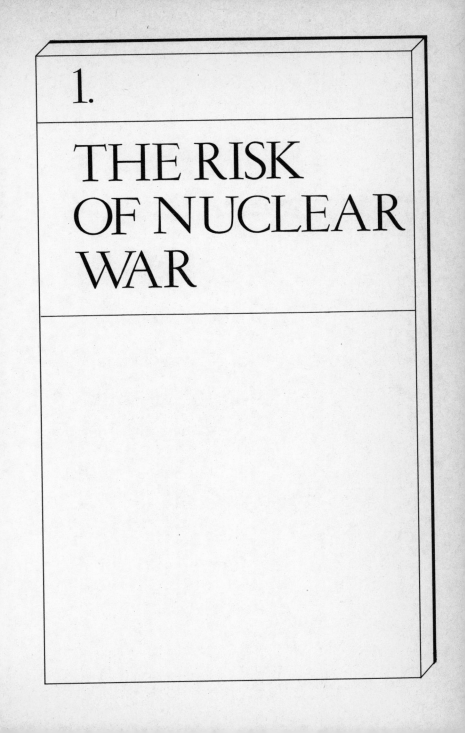

1.

THE RISK OF NUCLEAR WAR

In the nearly fifty years since Albert Einstein sent his historical letter to President Roosevelt warning him that it was essential that the United States move quickly to develop the nuclear bomb, the world's inventory of such weapons has increased from zero to fifty thousand. On average, each of them has a destructive power thirty times that of the Hiroshima bomb. A few hundred of the fifty thousand could destroy not only the United States, the Soviet Union, and their allies, but, through atmospheric effects, a major part of the rest of the world as well.

The weapons are widely deployed. They are supported by war-fighting strategies. Detailed war plans for their use are in the hands of the field commanders. And the troops of each side routinely undertake exercises specifically designed to prepare for that use. General Bernard Rogers, the Supreme Allied Commander of NATO forces in Europe, has said it is likely that in the early hours of a military conflict in Western Europe, NATO commanders would in fact ask for the authority to initiate such use.

This situation has evolved over the years through a series of incremental decisions. I myself participated in many of them. Each of the decisions, taken by itself, appeared rational or inescapable. But the fact is that they were made without reference to any overall master plan or long-term objective. They have led to nuclear arsenals and nuclear war plans that few of the participants either anticipated or would, in retrospect, wish to support.

Because we lack a long-run plan for the nuclear age, the number of weapons continues to multiply. And now we appear on the verge of an escalation of the arms race that will not only place weapons in space, but will seriously increase the risk that one or the other of the adversaries will be tempted in a period of tension to initiate a preemptive nuclear strike before the opponent can get in the first blow.

Although four decades have passed without the use of nuclear weapons in combat, and though it is clear that both the United States and the USSR are aware of the dangers of nuclear war, it is equally true that for thousands of years the human race has engaged in war. There is no sign that this is about to change. And history is replete with examples of occasions in such wars when emotions have taken hold and replaced reason.

I do not believe the Soviet Union wants war with the West. And certainly the West will not attack the USSR or its allies. But dangerous frictions between the Warsaw Pact and NATO have developed in the past and are likely to do so in the future. If deterrence fails and conflict develops, the present U.S. and NATO strategy carries with it a high risk that Western civilization will be destroyed.

During the seven years I served as Secretary of Defense, confrontations carrying a serious risk of military conflict developed on three separate occasions: over Berlin in August of 1961, over the introduction of Soviet missiles into Cuba in October of 1962, and in the Middle East in June of 1967. In none of these cases did either side want war. In each of them we came perilously close to it.

The Berlin crisis began, I believe, with the Bay of Pigs invasion in April 1961. Seventy days after assuming office President Kennedy accepted the advice of the Central Intelligence Agency, supported by every one of his senior advisors in the Administration, including myself, to put into effect a plan for the invasion and liberation of Cuba on which the Agency had been working for several years. The result, closely observed by the Soviet Union, can only be described as a debacle.

Less than two months later the President met with Soviet leader Nikita Khrushchev in Vienna. Khrushchev, conditioned perhaps by the Administration's mismanagement of the Cuban operations, judged Kennedy to be both inexperienced and soft.

Based on that judgment, he apparently concluded that the Soviet Union, with little risk, could remove West Berlin from the control of the West. He set out to do so.

- The Soviets began by dropping chaff (similar to large masses of tinfoil) in the air corridors serving Berlin. This disrupted navigational equipment and hindered Western resupply of the city by air.
- NATO responded by increasing the number of convoys traveling to Berlin along the ground corridors that traverse East Germany.
- The Soviets instructed the East Germans to stop the convoys at the checkpoints on the border between the two Germanys.
- The Allies reinforced the convoys with military escorts and were prepared, if necessary, to force their way past the border guards.
- Some time later the East Germans allowed a convoy with military escort to enter the ground corridor but refused it permission to exit into West Berlin. Ultimately, we forced its release, but it was clear the Soviets intended to escalate the conflict.

I asked a senior NATO commander what further moves we should expect and how we should respond. He said the Soviets would probably do *a* and we *b;* they *c* and we *d;* they *e* and we *f;* and then they would be forced to *g.* And when I said, "What do we do then?" he replied, "We should use nuclear weapons." When I asked how he expected the Soviets to respond, he said, "With nuclear weapons."

In the event, of course, we did no such thing. We called up reserves, rushed additional forces to Europe, and made clear our firm intention to defend West Berlin. At that point the threat receded. But if the Soviets had continued to escalate their threats to Berlin, or if either side had interpreted actions by the other as preparations for full-scale attack, who can say what might finally have happened?

Fourteen months later we again found ourselves in a confrontation with the Soviets.

On October 14, 1962, a U-2 aircraft, flying a reconnaissance mission, obtained photographic evidence that the USSR had moved nuclear-tipped ballistic missiles into Cuba. Their range would permit them to attack the most heavily populated regions on the East Coast.

It is true that at the time we had a strategic nuclear force of approximately five thousand warheads compared to the Soviet's three hundred. But despite this numerical superiority of seventeen to one, we did not believe we had a capability to launch a successful "first strike" against the USSR.* It is possible, nevertheless, that the Soviets feared we might do so.

---

*In this book I use the term "first strike" to denote a nuclear attack so powerful as to leave one's opponent with forces which are insufficient to inflict substantial damage on the attacker. In contrast, the term "first use" refers to the initial use of nuclear weapons in a military conflict. It may have more limited objectives than a first strike, e.g., the defeat of an enemy tank attack.

Driven by that fear, they may have sought to increase the size of their retaliatory forces by moving relatively short-range missiles from Soviet soil to Cuba, thereby increasing the number of weapons that threatened our shores.

In any event, because the United States had been "deterred" from a first strike by the force balances that had existed prior to the introduction of the weapons into Cuba, that action, in the opinion of many in the Administration, did not change the military balance. It did, however, represent a political move that, it was believed, must be reversed.

There were two schools of thought on how this should be done.

One group, which included the majority of President Kennedy's advisors, believed we should seek to destroy the missiles by an air attack. It was recognized that such an attack would almost certainly require a follow-up ground invasion that might result in twenty-five thousand U.S. casualties and a corresponding number of Cubans dead or wounded. Further, it was believed that while our military superiority in the hemisphere would assure the success of the air attacks and the land invasion, the Soviet Union would very likely respond by military action against the flanks or even the center of NATO.

Those who opposed the air attacks recommended a quarantine designed to prevent Soviet resupply of Cuba until the missiles were withdrawn.

The President chose the second option.

The quarantine was put in place on October 24. On October 25 a Soviet tanker approached the designated quarantine line and refused to stop despite the presence of a U.S. destroyer (the *Joseph P. Kennedy, Jr.*) on its quarter. The immediate question was, How should the United States react? Some proposed that we force the vessel to halt by gunfire. Others suggested that we not push the Soviets into a corner at that stage but give their leadership more opportunity to react to our position and ample time to communicate their decision to all their vessels at sea.

The tanker was allowed to "pass through" the line.

Diplomatic exchanges continued.

On Friday evening, October 26, we received the most extraordinary diplomatic message I have ever seen. The teletype was six or seven feet in length. It was a long, rambling message signed by Khrushchev. The text had obviously been dictated by a man under intense emotional pressure. Khrushchev said, in effect, "We are both engaged in a tug-of-war, pulling on either end of a rope and thereby tying a knot that, once tied, neither of us will ever be able to undo." He was saying that events, were they to continue, would inevitably lead to war. And he added, "If war should break out, it would not be in our power to stop it—war ends when it has rolled through cities and villages, everywhere sowing death and destruction."

On Saturday morning a second message arrived. It was tougher, more coldly threatening, and clearly the reflection of a group decision rather than the words of a single individual.

Tensions continued to rise that Saturday. New photographs suggested that the Soviets were continuing work on installing the missiles. U.S. forces in Florida prepared for an invasion of Cuba. Another Soviet ship was heading toward the quarantine line. Meanwhile, our naval antisubmarine forces in the Caribbean were closely tracking Soviet submarines and had forced five or six of them to surface near the quarantine zone.

We then learned that one of our U-2 planes had been shot down over Cuba by a Soviet surface-to-air missile. The pilot was killed. A second U-2, flying from Alaska to the North Pole, strayed over Soviet territory and drew a crowd of Soviet fighter planes before regaining its course.

Against this background we chose to reply to Khrushchev's original, less threatening communication, emphasizing that we had no intention of invading Cuba if the Soviet offensive forces were removed from the hemisphere. But we made clear that if they were not removed, further action by the United States would follow.

I will not speculate on what that further action might have been, but I do know that as I left the White House and walked through the garden to my car to return to the Pentagon on that beautiful fall evening, I feared I might never live to see another Saturday night.

I do not wish to indicate that there was the slightest possibility that, had military action followed, we would have initiated the use of nuclear weapons. Nor do I wish to suggest that we believed the Politburo, even in the face of U.S. air and sea attacks, would have authorized launching of the Cuban-based nuclear missiles against our East Coast cities. But who could say that with his forces about to be destroyed, a Soviet or Cuban lieutenant on the scene would not have given the order to fire?

On Sunday Khrushchev informed the President he had issued orders to dismantle the missile bases and remove the missiles and bomber aircraft from Cuba.

The third serious confrontation with the Soviets arose over the Middle East.

Early in June 1967 it was apparent to both the British and ourselves that the Egyptians, who had been receiving Soviet military support and who were assisted by Soviet military advisors, were preparing to attack Israel. The Israelis, having knowledge of Egypt's preparations, were moving toward "preemption," which President Johnson unsuccessfully sought to prevent. In the early morning hours of June 5, Israel attacked and inflicted severe losses on the Egyptian forces.

At seven the next morning, as was my custom, I arrived at the Pentagon. Soon after, the general on duty in the War Room called to report that Soviet Prime Minister Aleksei Kosygin wished to talk with President Johnson on the "Hot Line," the direct teletype link between Washington and Moscow. The general asked what response he should make. I said, "Why are you calling me?" He replied that the Hot Line ends at the Pentagon.

It may sound absurd, but I had been Secretary for three years since the Hot Line had been installed, and because it had never been used, I was not aware that the teletype facility terminated below my office. In shock and surprise I told the general that we were spending some tens of billions of dollars a year on defense and, within the next fifteen minutes, he had better find a way to divert a few of those dollars to facilitate an extension of the teletype to the White House.

I then called the President, knowing that he would probably be asleep and that the Air Force sergeant who monitored the calls during the night would answer the phone. The sergeant did answer. I said I wanted to speak to the President. He replied that the President was asleep. I said, "I know that, but tell him that Secretary McNamara asks that he be awakened." The sergeant did. The President came to the phone, and in a sleepy, gruff voice said, "Goddamn it, Bob, what is the problem?" I said, "Prime Minister Kosygin wants to talk to you on the Hot Line. How should I reply?"

The President, of course, moved quickly to join Dean Rusk and me in the Situation Room to receive the message. Kosygin said he would work for a cease-fire. We replied we would do the same.

While we sought a negotiated settlement, the Israelis continued to advance. By June 8 they had reached cease-fire agreements with Jordan and Egypt, but they continued fighting with Syria in the Golan Heights. In the early hours of June 10 we learned that Israel was ready to terminate hostilities with Syria. We believed that an end to the war was in sight.

Suddenly, Kosygin was calling again on the Hot Line, but this time the message reflected anger and threats. It said, in effect, "If you want war, you will get war."

Kosygin may have been reacting to our earlier actions. Fearing that the Soviet Union might seek to help Egypt avenge its defeat by launching a counterattack on Israel, we had ordered the U.S. Sixth Fleet—which had been conducting training exercises in the Mediterranean and was steaming West toward Gibraltar—to reverse course and steam East. Our intention had been to put the task force in a position to defend Israel. But the Soviets may have believed we were preparing to attack Egypt.

In the face of Kosygin's threat, the President decided we had to take a tough stance. He instructed me to move the Sixth Fleet closer to the Syrian coast in order to signal unmistakably our determination to oppose any attack on Israel.

The dialogue continued over the Hot Line and eventually a cease-fire was agreed upon. But once again the superpowers had moved close to confrontation. If the Israeli-Syrian cease-fire had failed, superpower military intervention in the region would have become a reality.

In no one of the three incidents did either side intend to act in a way that would lead to military conflict, but on each of the occasions lack of information, misinformation, and misjudgments led to confrontation. And in each of them, as the crisis evolved, tensions heightened, emotions rose, and the danger of irrational decisions increased.

It is correct to say that no well-informed, coolly rational political or military leader is likely to initiate the use of nuclear weapons. But political and military leaders, in moments of severe crisis, are likely to be neither well informed nor coolly rational.

In 1962 President Kennedy insisted that each member of the National Security Council read Barbara Tuchman's *The Guns of August.* The book is the story of how the nations of Europe inadvertently blundered into World War I. The author begins by quoting Bismarck's comment that "some damned foolish thing in the Balkans" would ignite the next war. She then relates the series of steps—following the assassination on June 28, 1914, of the Austrian heir apparent, Archduke Franz Ferdinand, by Serbian nationalists—each small and insignificant in itself, that led to the most appalling military conflict in the history of the world. Time and again, at the brink of hostilities, the chiefs of state tried to pull back, but the momentum of events dragged them forward.

President Kennedy reminded us of the 1914 conversation between two German chancellors on the origins of that war. One asked, "How did it happen?" and his successor replied, "Ah, if we only knew." It was Kennedy's way of stressing the constant danger of miscalculation.

Today we face a future in which for decades we must contemplate continuing confrontation between East and West. Any one of these confrontations can escalate, through miscalculation, into military conflict. And that conflict will be between blocs that possess fifty thousand nuclear warheads— warheads that are deployed on the battlefields and integrated into the war plans. A single nuclear-armed submarine of either side could unleash more firepower than man has shot against man throughout history.

In the tense atmosphere of a crisis, each side will feel pressure to delegate authority to fire nuclear weapons to battlefield commanders. As the likelihood of attack increases, these commanders will face a desperate dilemma: use them or lose them.

And because the strategic nuclear forces, and the complex systems designed to command and control them, are perceived by many to be vulnerable to a preemptive attack, they will argue the advantage of a preemptive strike.

The risk that military conflict will quickly evolve into nuclear war, leading to certain destruction of our civilization, is far greater than I am willing to accept on military, political, or moral grounds. It is far greater than I am prepared to pass on to my children or grandchildren.

What, if anything, can be done to eliminate that risk, or, at a minimum, reduce it to more tolerable levels in the second half of this first century of the nuclear age?

Should we not set that as our objective and develop a plan for achieving it? Such a plan would guide the evolution of military strategy, the preparation of war plans, the development of nuclear weapons, the procurement and deployment of nuclear forces, and the negotiation of arms control agreements.

The formulation of such a plan will be the objective of this book.

The first half—Chapters 2 and 3—will review the evolution of U.S. and Soviet nuclear forces and strategy during the period since the Fermi experimental pile went critical in December 1942. It will describe the force balance today. It will examine each side's perceptions and misperceptions of that balance. It will look at potential future force developments. And it will consider how these will affect crisis stability.

The second half of the book—Chapters 4 and 5—will discuss alternative ways of reducing the risk of nuclear war in the decades that lie ahead:

- Achieving political reconciliation between the parties.
- Eliminating all nuclear weapons by negotiations, as proposed by General Secretary Gorbachev.

- Substituting "defensive" forces for our existing offensive forces, thereby permitting the elimination of all nuclear weapons, as proposed by President Reagan.
- "Strengthening" our deterrent by adding defensive forces to the offense, as suggested by such security experts as Henry Kissinger, Zbigniew Brzezinski, and Max Kampelman.
- Accepting the proposition that nuclear warheads are not military weapons in the traditional sense and therefore serve no military purpose other than to deter one's opponent from their use. Such a view would require fundamental adjustments in NATO's strategy, war plans, and conventional force levels; weapons development programs; and arms control agreements.

The book will conclude that this last approach offers the opportunity for laying a foundation for entering the twenty-first century with a totally different nuclear strategy, one of mutual security instead of war-fighting; with vastly smaller nuclear forces, perhaps one thousand weapons in place of fifty thousand; and with a dramatically lower risk that our civilization will be destroyed by nuclear war.

2.

THE FIRST HALF CENTURY OF THE NUCLEAR AGE

Evolution of U.S. and Soviet Nuclear Forces and Strategy, 1940–1990

N uclear weapons, Albert Einstein said, changed every-
thing except our mode of thinking. The destructive-
ness of the nuclear bomb is far beyond any other
power unleashed by humanity. Yet a persistent theme of the
nuclear age has been efforts by strategists of both East and
West to treat these awesome devices as weapons available for
use like other weapons.

In the 1950s the United States had plans to use its nuclear
bombs very much as it had conducted strategic bombing with
conventional explosives during World War II—to destroy cities and industrial targets that comprised the enemy's "war-
making capacity."

By the end of the decade, technological developments led
to a shift in our strategy. Sophisticated reconnaissance aircraft
and satellites were providing increasingly detailed information
about the location and structure of Soviet military targets.
Moreover, the development of ballistic missiles meant that
nuclear explosives could be delivered with great accuracy.

As a result, U.S. strategists attempted to formulate plans for
the use of nuclear weapons that could move our strategy away
from the targeting of Soviet cities and toward targeting of
military forces.

The belief that the United States should develop forces and
plans for fighting a nuclear war and targeting enemy forces
has persisted to the present day. This trend has culminated
in the view of the Defense Department under Secretary of

Defense Caspar Weinberger that the United States could actually achieve victory in such a war. According to Weinberger's 1984–88 defense guidance document, "Should deterrence fail and strategic nuclear war with the USSR occur, the United States must prevail and be able to force the Soviet Union to seek earliest termination of hostilities on terms favorable to the United States."

Today eleven thousand U.S. strategic warheads are poised against some five thousand targets. And NATO's war plans are based on early first use of some five thousand tactical nuclear weapons in response to a Soviet conventional attack. Nuclear weapons are deployed with U.S. and Soviet forces all over the world. Although both sides are aware that a nuclear war that engaged even a small fraction of their arsenals would be an unmitigated disaster, each is vigorously deploying and developing new weapons systems that the opponent will view as highly threatening.

How we got into this dangerous situation is perhaps best understood by taking a closer look at the development of nuclear forces and strategy as they related to the situation in Europe.

Throughout the postwar period the security of Europe has been the centerpiece of U.S. foreign policy; it is likely to remain so indefinitely. In no other region have the two great powers deployed so many nuclear weapons. In no other part of the world are military doctrines that specify the use of nuclear weapons granted such wide-ranging credibility.

The use of nuclear weapons has been an integral part of NATO's military strategy virtually since the inception of the Alliance.

THE DEVELOPMENT OF NATO'S FORCE STRUCTURE

Shortly after the North Atlantic Treaty was ratified in 1949, estimates were made of the size of the Soviet military threat as a basis for developing NATO's military strategy and force structure. Believing that the USSR could muster as many as 175 divisions against Western Europe, NATO military planners concluded that the Alliance would require 96 of its own divisions—which were larger than those of the Soviet Union —in order to mount an adequate defense. This estimate was accepted by the NATO ministers in February 1952 at their annual meeting in Lisbon.

It soon became clear, however, that the member nations were not willing to meet these so-called Lisbon force goals. Instead, the Alliance turned consciously to nuclear weapons as a substitute for the financial and manpower sacrifices which would have been necessary to mount an adequate conventional defense.

That budgetary considerations were a key factor in NATO's decision to rely on nuclear weapons is evident from the following statement by then Secretary of State John Foster Dulles.

The total cost of our security efforts (and those of our Allies) . . . could not be continued long without grave budgetary, economic, and social consequences. But before military planning could be changed the President and his advisers . . . had to make some basic policy decisions. This has been done. The basic decision was to depend primarily upon a greater [nuclear] capacity to retaliate instantly by means and at places of our own choosing. As a result it is now possible to get and to share more basic security at less cost.

Nor was this new emphasis only rhetorical. A presidential directive (NSC-162/2) ordered the Joint Chiefs of Staff to plan on using nuclear armaments whenever it would be to the United States' advantage to do so. Changes were made in the organization and plans of the U.S. Army so that it would be better able to fight on nuclear battlefields. By late 1953 substantial numbers of tactical nuclear weapons—artillery shells, bombs, short-range missiles, nuclear mines, and others—were beginning to be deployed in Europe. The buildup of NATO tactical nuclear weapons continued steadily, peaking in the mid-1960s at around seven thousand. Although large numbers of conventional forces were retained on the continent, until the early 1960s their only purpose was seen to be to contain an attack long enough for nuclear strikes to defeat the aggressor. Nuclear weapons were considered the "real" deterrent. Many of these systems were short-range and deployed near the borders between NATO and Warsaw Pact countries. By deployment of these systems near the border, NATO intended to signal clearly to the Soviets that any conventional attack by Warsaw Pact forces would quickly involve NATO nuclear forces.

If there were any doubts about the seriousness of NATO's nuclear threats in the 1950s, they should have been dispelled by the following statement by General Bernard Montgomery, the deputy supreme allied commander in Europe, who said in late 1954:

I want to make it absolutely clear that we at SHAPE are basing all our operational planning on using atomic and thermonuclear weapons in our own defense. With us it is no longer "they may possibly be used," it is very definite "they will be used, if we are attacked."

By December 1954 the NATO ministers felt comfortable enough with the nuclear strategy to reduce the force level objective from ninety-six to thirty active divisions. Two years later, the Alliance formally adopted the policy of "massive retaliation" in a document known as MC 14/2.

Whether the balance of nuclear forces between the Warsaw Pact and NATO, as it was developing during the mid-1950s, justified adoption of NATO's nuclear strategy is arguable. But its merit had become questionable to many by the early 1960s. Soon after taking office in January 1961, the Kennedy Administration began a detailed analysis of the policy's strengths and weaknesses.

These studies revealed two major deficiencies in the reasoning that had led to the adoption of MC 14/2: (1) the relative balance of NATO and Warsaw Pact conventional forces was far less unfavorable from a Western perspective than had been assumed (the power of Soviet forces had been overestimated and that of NATO forces underestimated); and (2) there was great uncertainty as to whether and, if so, how nuclear weapons could be used to NATO's advantage.

President Kennedy, therefore, authorized me as Secretary of Defense to propose, at a meeting of the NATO ministers in Athens in May 1962, to substitute a strategy of "flexible response" for the existing doctrine of "massive retaliation."

The new strategy required a buildup of NATO's conventional forces, but on a scale that we believed to be practical on both financial and political grounds. Instead of the early massive use of nuclear weapons, it permitted a substantial raising of the nuclear threshold by planning for the critical initial responses to Soviet aggression to be made by conventional forces alone. The strategy was based on the expectation that NATO's conventional capabilities could be improved sufficiently so that the use of nuclear weapons would be unnecessary. But, under the new doctrine, even if this expectation turned out to be false, any use of nuclear weapons would be "late and limited."

Our proposal of the new strategy was the result of the recognition by U.S. civilian and military officials that NATO's vastly superior nuclear capabilities, measured in terms of numbers of weapons, did not translate into usable military power. Moreover, we understood that the initial use of even a small number of strategic or tactical nuclear weapons implied risks that could threaten the very survival of the nation. Consequently, we, in effect, proposed confining nuclear weapons to only two roles in the NATO context: deterring the Soviet's initiation of nuclear war; and as a weapon of last resort, if conventional defense failed, to persuade the aggressor to terminate the conflict on acceptable terms.

The proposed change in NATO's strategy met with strong opposition.

Some opponents argued that the United States was seeking to "decouple" itself from the defense of Europe. These critics shared our view that a "tactical" nuclear war in Europe would quickly escalate to a strategic exchange involving the U.S. and Soviet homelands, but they saw this danger as the primary factor that deterred Soviet aggression. Any reduction in this prospect, they argued, might cause the Soviets to believe the hostilities could be confined to Central Europe, and thus tempt them into adventures.

Other critics maintained that the proposed buildup of NATO's conventional forces was totally beyond what the Alliance would be willing to support. Still others argued that we had greatly exaggerated the dangers of limited uses of nuclear weapons.

The argument raged for five years. It was not until 1967 that NATO adopted the strategy of flexible response, inscribing it in a document known as MC 14/3.

The revised strategy proposed to deter aggression by maintaining forces adequate to counter an attack at whatever level the aggressor chose to fight. Should such a direct confrontation not prove successful, the strategy proposed to escalate as necessary, including the initial use of nuclear weapons, forcing the aggressor to confront costs and risks disproportionate to his initial objectives. At all times, however, the flexible-response strategy specified that efforts should be made to control the scope and intensity of combat. Thus, for example, initial nuclear attacks presumably would be made by short-range tactical systems in an attempt to confine the effects of nuclear warfare to the battlefield. Even so, the strategy retained the ultimate escalatory threat of a strategic exchange between U.S. and Soviet homelands to make clear the final magnitude of the dangers being contemplated.

Flexible response has remained NATO's official doctrine for nearly twenty years. Its essential element, however—building sufficient conventional capabilities to offset those of the Warsaw Pact—has never been achieved. Indeed, during the late 1960s and early 1970s, the Alliance may have fallen farther behind its opponent. Although NATO has made considerable strides in improving its conventional posture in more recent years, most military experts believe that the conventional balance continues to favor the Warsaw Pact; they thus conclude an attack by Soviet conventional forces would require the use of nuclear weapons, most likely within a matter of hours. Contrary to the understanding of the American public, NATO's operational war plans reflect this belief. The substantial raising of the nuclear threshold, as was envisioned when flexible response was first conceived, has not become a reality.

THE EVOLUTION OF SOVIET NUCLEAR STRATEGY

Before turning to the question of whether NATO can initiate the use of nuclear weapons—in response to a Soviet attack—with benefit to the Alliance, I should perhaps comment on the evolution of Soviet nuclear strategy over the past three decades.

For much of the postwar period, Soviet military doctrine appears to have assumed that war between the great powers would include the use of nuclear weapons. Soviet publications stressed the use of both long- and intermediate-range nuclear weapons, in the initial hours of a conflict, to destroy concentrations of enemy forces and the ports, airfields, and other facilities necessary to support military operations. And these publications emphasized as well the use of tactical nuclear weapons on the battlefield.

The way that Soviet soldiers trained, the protective clothing and decontamination equipment with which they were equipped, and the nature of their military exercises—which for years always included a nuclear phase—suggested that the written expressions of Soviet military doctrine constituted deadly serious descriptions of the way the USSR planned to fight the next war.

In fact, until the mid-1960s, writings of Soviet military officials consistently maintained that the only conflict possible between the great powers was an all-out nuclear war. They asserted, moreover, that it was possible to prevail in such a conflict, and they urged the military and social preparations necessary to ensure that the USSR emerged triumphant from any nuclear conflict. It was these writings that, in the late 1970s, were invoked repeatedly by U.S. opponents of nuclear arms control in the debate on the SALT II Treaty.

By that time, however, this portrayal of Soviet military doctrine was becoming badly out-of-date.

Official Soviet doctrine changed slightly in the mid-1960s as Soviet writers began to admit the possibility of a "war by stages" in Europe, in which the first phase would be a conventional one. Although they asserted that this initial stage would be very short, and further noted that the conflict "inevitably" would escalate to all-out nuclear war, the previous doctrinal rigidity had been broken.

Soviet experts and military officials debated the inevitability of nuclear escalation throughout the 1960s and much of the 1970s. By the time of a famous speech of Leonid Brezhnev at Tula in 1977, the question seems to have been settled. Soviet theorists then admitted the possibility of a major protracted war between East and West in which nuclear weapons would not be used.

Indeed, the Soviets now officially maintain that they would not be the first to make use of nuclear weapons. This declaration was first officially articulated in a message from Brezhnev to the United Nations General Assembly on June 12, 1982: "The Union of Soviet Socialist Republics assumes an obligation not to be the first to use nuclear weapons." In the same year, Defense Minister Dmitri Ustinov stated, "Only extraordinary circumstances—a direct nuclear aggression against the Soviet state or its allies—can compel us to resort to a retaliatory nuclear strike as a last means of self-defense." These statements represented a change in position for the USSR. Previously, Soviet spokesmen had only been willing to say that they would not use nuclear weapons against nonnuclear powers.

Along with this shift has come the explicit and repeated renunciation of what Soviet spokesmen had declared for more than two decades: that it was possible to fight and win a nuclear war. All Soviet writers and political leaders addressing this question now solemnly declare that "there will be no victors in a nuclear war."

Does this doctrinal shift suggest that the USSR is no longer prepared for nuclear war in Europe? Certainly not. In addition to the deployment of intermediate-range SS-20 missiles, the Soviets are busily modernizing their shorter-range nuclear-armed missiles in Europe (SS-21s, SS-22s, and SS-23s). Two types of artillery tubes capable of firing nuclear charges have been seen with Soviet units in Eastern Europe in larger numbers in recent years. And there are now many more aircraft capable of delivering nuclear bombs deployed with Soviet forces in Europe than was the case not many years ago.

The USSR is obviously prepared to respond if NATO chooses to initiate nuclear war. I turn, then, to the question of whether NATO can initiate the use of nuclear weapons, in response to a Soviet conventional attack, with benefit to the Alliance.

AN EVALUATION OF PLANS FOR THE USE OF NUCLEAR WEAPONS

Doubts about the wisdom of NATO's strategy of flexible response, never far from the surface, emerged as a major issue in the late 1970s. Debate has intensified in the ensuing years. The debate hinges on assessment of the military value of nuclear weapons.

The nuclear balance has changed substantially since the Kennedy Administration first proposed a strategy of flexible response. Both sides have virtually completely refurbished their inventories, increasing the number of weapons of all three types—battlefield, intermediate-range, and strategic—while vastly improving the performance characteristics of both the weapons themselves and their delivery systems. Because the Soviet Union was so far behind the United States in the early 1960s, the quantitative changes, at least, appear to have been more favorable for the USSR. The ratio of warheads on strategic launchers, for example, has shifted from a ten-to-one U.S. advantage in 1965 to a far more modest eleven-to-ten advantage at present. Table 1 summarizes the strategic nuclear warhead inventories of the two sides from 1965 to 1985 (see Appendix IV for a breakdown by type).

TABLE 1. STRATEGIC NUCLEAR WARHEADS

	1965	1970	1975	1980	1985
U.S.	5,550	4,000	8,500	10,100	11,200
Soviet Union	600	1,800	2,800	6,000	9,900

As the Soviet Union moved toward, and then achieved, rough parity in strategic, intermediate-range, and tactical nuclear forces, a crucial element of the flexible-response strategy became less and less credible.

It will be recalled that the strategy calls for the Alliance to initiate nuclear war with battlefield weapons if conventional defenses fail and to escalate the type of nuclear weapons used (and therefore the targets of those weapons), as necessary, up to and including the use of strategic forces against targets in the USSR itself. Given the tremendous devastation which those Soviet strategic forces that survived a U.S. first strike would now be able to inflict on this country, it is difficult to imagine any U.S. President, under any circumstances, initiating a strategic strike except in retaliation against a Soviet nuclear strike. It is this reasoning which led to a much-criticized statement by Henry Kissinger in Brussels in 1979. He made clear he did not believe the U.S. would ever initiate a nuclear strike against the Soviet Union. Kissinger's speech was criticized not for its logic, only for its frankness.

In short, a key element of the flexible-response strategy has been overtaken by a change in the physical realities of the nuclear balance. With huge survivable arsenals on both sides, the likelihood that a strategic attack would be met in kind is very great indeed. Thus, strategic nuclear weapons have lost whatever military utility may once have been attributed to them. Their sole purpose, at present, is to deter the other side's first use of its strategic forces.

Thus, given that NATO would not be the first to use strategic nuclear weapons, is it conceivable that the first use of tactical weapons would be to its military advantage?

The roughly five thousand NATO nuclear weapons now deployed in Europe consist of warheads for air-defense missiles, nuclear mines (known as atomic demolition munitions), warheads for shorter-range missiles, nuclear bombs, and nuclear-armed artillery shells. A rough estimate of the distribution of these weapons is shown in Table 2.*

TABLE 2. U.S. NUCLEAR WARHEADS LOCATED IN EUROPE IN 1985

Bombs to be delivered by aircraft	1,075
Artillery shells (203mm and 155mm)	1,660
Missiles—Pershing Ia	72
Lance and Honest John	895
Pershing II	108
Cruise missile	128
Air defense and atomic demolition charges	870
Total	4,808

*Reductions are being made in NATO's tactical nuclear forces in Europe, but the figures are roughly representative of present levels.

According to these figures, nuclear artillery shells comprise the largest portion of the stockpile, about one-third of the total. They are also the weapons which cause the greatest worry.

There are two types of nuclear artillery shells in the NATO inventory: those for 155mm howitzers and those for 203mm cannons. Both the howitzers and cannons are dual-capable; they can be used to fire shells containing conventional explosives as well as nuclear weapons. The precise ranges of these systems are classified, but most accounts put them at around ten miles. Because of the short range of nuclear artillery, the guns and their nuclear shells tend to be deployed close to the potential front lines of any conflict in Europe—there are, in effect, approximately two thousand short-range nuclear warheads concentrated at a few sites close to the German border.

Atomic demolition munitions (ADMs) also raise particular concerns. Intended to block mountain passes and other "choke points" on potential Soviet invasion routes, their effects would be felt on NATO territory. Moreover, to be effective they would have to be emplaced before a war actually began. Indications that NATO was preparing to emplace ADMs could aggravate a crisis and would probably contribute to the likelihood of the war starting. At the same time, because ADMs would have to be used at the very onset of the conflict, their use would mean that NATO had not tested the ability of its conventional forces to contain a Warsaw Pact invasion.

Similar problems beset nuclear-armed air defense systems. They are intended for use at the onset of a conflict—to disrupt the large-scale air attacks that would accompany a Warsaw Pact invasion—thus negating the strategy of flexible response.

In an acute crisis in which the risk of war seemed to be rising, these characteristics of nuclear artillery, mines, and air defense systems would be likely to lead to pressures on

NATO's political leaders, particularly the U.S. President, to delegate the authority to release these weapons to the military commanders on the scene. Whether such authority was delegated or not, it is these characteristics—most importantly the vulnerability of NATO's nuclear artillery—that lead many observers to predict that the Alliance would use tactical nuclear weapons within hours of the start of a war in Europe. Given the vulnerability of these systems near the border and NATO's declared plans to use them early, the Soviets would have tremendous incentive to attack them quickly with conventional weapons. NATO would be likely to face the choice of either using its battlefield nuclear weapons or seeing them overrun or destroyed by the enemy.

In terms of their military utility, NATO has not found it possible to develop plans for the use of nuclear artillery that would both assure a clear advantage to the Alliance and at the same time avoid the very high risk of escalating to all-out nuclear war.

Current guidelines on the initial use of nuclear weapons date from the early 1970s. A former member of the High Level Group, a special official committee established by NATO in 1978 to examine the Alliance's nuclear posture, stated that despite discussions lasting for years, "NATO has not yet managed to agree on guidelines for the follow-on use of nuclear weapons if a first attempt to communicate NATO's intentions through a controlled demonstrative use did not succeed in persuading the adversary to halt hostilities."

Two problems stand in the way.

First, since the assumption is made that NATO will be responding to a Warsaw Pact invasion of Western Europe, and since the artillery has short range, the nuclear explosions would occur on NATO's own territory. If a substantial portion of the two thousand nuclear artillery shells were fired, not only would the Warsaw Pact likely suffer heavy casualties among its military personnel, but large numbers of NATO's civilian and military personnel also would be killed and injured. There also would be considerable damage to property, farmland, and urban areas.

Moreover, there is no reason to believe that the Warsaw Pact, now possessing tactical and intermediate-range nuclear forces at least comparable to those of NATO, would not respond to NATO's initiation of nuclear war with major nuclear attacks of its own. These attacks would probably seek most importantly to reduce NATO's ability to fight nuclear war by destroying command and control facilities; nuclear weapons storage sites; and the aircraft, missiles, and artillery that would deliver NATO's nuclear weapons. Direct support facilities such as ports and airfields would likely also be attacked in the initial Warsaw Pact nuclear offensive. Thus, the war would escalate from the battlefield to the rest of Western Europe (and probably to Eastern Europe as well, as NATO retaliated).

What would be the consequences of such a conflict? In 1955 an exercise called Carte Blanche simulated the use of 335 nuclear weapons, 80 percent of which were assumed to detonate on German territory. In terms of immediate casualties (ignoring the victims of radiation disease, and so forth), it was estimated that between 1.5 and 1.7 million people would die and another 3.5 million would be wounded—more than five times the German civilian casualties in World War II—in the first two days.

This exercise prompted Helmut Schmidt to remark that the use of tactical nuclear weapons "will not defend Europe, but destroy it."

Additional studies throughout the 1960s confirmed these results. They prompted two of my former aides in the Pentagon to write in 1971: "Even under the most favorable assumptions, it appeared that between 2 and 20 million Europeans would be killed, with widespread damage to the economy of the affected area and a high risk of 100 million dead if the war escalated to attacks on cities."

Have the more modern weapons deployed on both sides in the 1970s changed the likely results of nuclear war in Europe? Not at all. A group of experts was assembled in 1980 by the UN Secretary General to study nuclear war. They simulated a conflict in which 1,500 nuclear artillery shells and 200 nuclear bombs were used by the two sides against each other's military targets. The experts concluded that as a result of such a conflict there would be a minimum of 5 to 6 million immediate civilian casualties and 400,000 military casualties, and that at least an additional 1.1 million civilians would suffer from radiation disease.

It should be remembered that all these scenarios, as horrible as they could be, involve the use of only a small portion of the tactical nuclear weapons deployed in Europe, and assume further that none of the thousands of nuclear warheads in the United States' and the Soviet Union's central strategic arsenals would be used. Yet portions of those central forces are intended for European contingencies: the United States has allocated four hundred of its submarine-based Poseidon warheads for use by NATO; the Soviet Union, it is believed, envisions as many as several hundred of its ICBMs being used against targets in Europe.

Is it realistic to expect that a nuclear war could be limited to the detonation of tens or even hundreds of nuclear weapons even though each side would have tens of thousands of weapons remaining available for use?

The answer is clearly no. Such an expectation requires the assumption that even though the initial strikes would have inflicted large-scale casualties and damage to both sides, one or the other—feeling disadvantaged—would give in. But under such circumstances, leaders on both sides would be under unimaginable pressure to avenge their losses and secure the interests being challenged. And each would fear that the opponent might launch a larger attack at any moment. Moreover, they would both be operating with only partial information because of the disruption of communications caused by the chaos on the battlefield (to say nothing of possible strikes against communications facilities). Under such conditions it is highly likely that rather than surrender, each side would launch a larger attack, hoping that this step would bring the action to a halt by causing the opponent to capitulate.

As I will discuss more fully in Chapter 4, it was assessments like these that led not only Field Marshal Lord Carver, but Lord Louis Mountbatten and several other of the eight retired Chiefs of the British Defence Staff as well, to indicate that under no circumstances would they have recommended that NATO initiate the use of nuclear weapons.

And it was similar considerations that led me to the same conclusions in 1961 and 1962.

It is inconceivable to me, as it has been to others who have studied the matter, that "limited" nuclear wars would remain limited—any decision to initiate the use of nuclear weapons would imply a high probability of the same cataclysmic consequences as a total nuclear exchange. In sum, I know of no plan that gives reasonable assurance that nuclear weapons can be used beneficially in NATO's defense. Yet NATO strategy continues to rely on the threat of first use of nuclear weapons.

Let me repeat, I do not believe that either the Soviet Union or the United States wishes war with the other. But, as I pointed out in Chapter 1, dangerous frictions between the Warsaw Pact and NATO have developed in the past and are likely to do so in the future. War is possible through misperception, misinformation, and miscalculation. If deterrence fails and conflict develops, NATO's first-use stance and stated strategy carry with them a high risk that Western civilization, as we know it, will be destroyed.

This is the unplanned—and to me unacceptable—result of the long series of incremental decisions taken by military and civilian leaders of East and West during the first half century of the nuclear age. Can we work ourselves out of this position during the next fifty years? Before considering that question, we should examine certain widely accepted views—views which I believe are misperceptions of reality—that tend to shape our answer.

3.

NUCLEAR MYTHS

Misperceptions That Endanger Our Security

M isperceptions of the nuclear balance between East and West, and of actions affecting that balance, are widespread, both in America and throughout the world. Let me illustrate by referring to several commonly held, but erroneous, views.

- The Soviets possess nuclear forces superior to our own.
- The Soviets possess, or are seeking to achieve, a first-strike capability.
- Regardless of American actions or restraint, the Soviets will continue to expand their nuclear power as quickly as they can for as long as they can.
- If the West mobilizes its technical resources, it can achieve and maintain a militarily significant lead over the Soviets.
- Given the political confrontation between East and West, the buildup of nuclear forces to their present level was inevitable.
- Arms control agreements are worthless—the Soviets cheat and their violations are undetectable.
- Arms control agreements have only led to Soviet advances.
- Nuclear weapons, even when militarily irrelevant, may serve political ends.

To label these beliefs as misperceptions is not to suggest that Soviet nuclear policies pose no threat. They represent a deadly danger. But to counter that threat effectively we must understand it. These misjudgments stand in the way.

THE SOVIETS HAVE NUCLEAR SUPERIORITY

The entire terminology of the nuclear "arms race" suggests that the United States is either ahead or behind, that there is a "winner" and a "loser." Americans have indicated, in poll after poll, that the United States should not seek to win the arms race. But neither are they prepared to lose—they will not tolerate Soviet superiority. When they are told the Soviet forces are superior, their concerns are legitimate and abiding. The important and difficult task is to know what nuclear superiority means and how to determine who, if anyone, has it.

Many prominent individuals claim that the Soviets are, in fact, "ahead." Jeane Kirkpatrick, former U.S. ambassador to the United Nations, wrote in January 1986:

> The most important development in international relations in 1985 . . . was the growing vulnerability of the United States. For the first time in American history an adversary has the ability to destroy our country. . . . The Soviet advantage in nuclear missiles is real and still growing. Our capacity for deterrence is minimal and still declining.

And Americans are familiar with President Reagan's views on the subject: "At the moment, I have to say that the United States . . . is still well behind the Soviet Union in literally every kind of offensive weapon." Paul Nitze, currently the President's arms control advisor, has warned: "The Soviet rulers do not want nuclear war. They believe the best way to avoid a nuclear war and still achieve their objectives is to have overwhelming superiority."

Statements like these seriously concern Americans, as well they should. But fortunately, the situation is quite different from what these quotations suggest. Consider, for example, Senator Sam Nunn's response to the President's statement: "Has the President been informed about the U.S. advantage in submarines, in aircraft carriers, in tactical aircraft, in rapid deployment capabilities, in sea-launched ballistic missiles, in cruise missiles, and in bombers? The President must know our weaknesses, but he must also be informed of our strengths." Americans should be informed as well. What, in fact, is the state of the nuclear balance between East and West?

The offensive forces of the two sides are shown in detail in Appendix III and are summarized in Table 3.

TABLE 3. U.S. AND SOVIET NUCLEAR ARSENALS IN 1985

| | Number of Missiles and Bombers | | Number of Warheads | |
	U.S.	Soviet	U.S.	Soviet
Long-range:				
ICBMS	1,023	1,398	2,126	6,420
Sub-launched missiles	690	967	5,728	2,887
Bombers	297	300	3,334	600
Subtotal			11,188	9,907
Intermediate-range missiles	236	514	236	1,435
Tactical nuclear weapons			9,500	8,432
Total*			20,924	19,774

*The totals exclude 10,000 warheads stockpiled but not deployed.

I recognize that simple numerical comparisons are incomplete approximations of relative military strengths. The figures, nonetheless, show near equality in both long-range and tactical warheads. More importantly, the totals far exceed the requirements of any conceivable war plan. In Churchill's famous phrase, the forces of each side are more than enough to make the rubble bounce many times over.

Recently, the Administration has suggested that not only do the Soviets enjoy superiority in offensive weapons, but in defensive systems as well. Defense Secretary Caspar Weinberger, for example, points out that over the last fifteen years the Soviets have spent "roughly as much on strategic defense systems as on their enormously expensive offensive strategic systems."

It is true that the Soviet Union has invested vast resources in defensive systems. But by far the greatest portion of that investment has been in bomber defenses. The United States stopped maintaining such forces in the 1960s at the beginning of the missile age. Today U.S. experts generally agree that the tens of billions of dollars the Soviets have spent on air defense in the past two decades have been largely wasted. As a matter of fact, I have never heard a senior U.S. military officer express any doubt whatsoever about our ability to penetrate Soviet air space. In 1985 Lawrence Gershwin of the Central Intelligence Agency testified before Congress that "against a combined attack of penetrating bombers and cruise missiles, Soviet air defenses during the next ten years probably would not be capable of inflicting sufficient losses to prevent large-scale damage to the USSR."

The Joint Chiefs of Staff are very clear on their views of the relative strengths of U.S. and Soviet nuclear forces. When asked if they would trade forces with the Soviets—both offensive and defensive—they have made it clear that they would not. General David Jones, former chairman of the Joint Chiefs of Staff, said in 1980, "I would not swap our present military capability with that of the Soviet Union." His view was confirmed by General John Vessey, JCS chairman from 1982 to 1985: "Overall, would I trade with Marshal Ogarkov (Chief of Staff of the Soviet Armed Forces)? Not on your life . . . I would not trade." The current JCS chairman, Admiral William Crowe, testified on February 5, 1986, that there was currently rough parity between the United States and the Soviet Union.

Despite the views of the chiefs and the force comparisons shown in the table, when the Reagan Administration first took office, as I will discuss more fully later in this chapter, it warned of a "window of vulnerability"—the danger that American land-based ballistic missiles could be destroyed in their silos by a surprise Soviet attack. But in 1983 the report of the President's Commission on Strategic Forces, headed by Lieutenant General Brent Scowcroft, concluded that the Administration's fears were unfounded and no such window of vulnerability existed.

Clearly, the military experts do not concur in the Administration's warnings of American inferiority. Does that mean the President and his associates have been intentionally misstating the facts?

I think not.

I feel quite certain that the President's warnings, though ill founded, have not been conscious attempts to mislead the public. Such mistaken judgments are not without precedent. John F. Kennedy, during his campaign for the presidency in 1960, also expressed serious concerns about a strategic gap— a missile gap—between the U.S. and Soviet forces. He based his statements on intelligence estimates from the Air Force. My first priority, therefore, after I took the oath of office as Secretary of Defense in January 1961, was to determine the size of that gap and to take immediate steps to close it. It took my deputy, Roswell Gilpatric, and me no more than three weeks to learn that indeed there was a gap in offensive warheads. However, as had been documented by the CIA, it was a gap very much in the favor of the United States (see Appendix IV). The Air Force, without any intention to deceive, had simply interpreted ambiguous data in ways that supported their weapons programs.

Misperceptions such as the mythical missile gap and the window of vulnerability can be very costly indeed. They can lead to inflated defense budgets, increased suspicions between East and West, and—in political or military crises—to misjudgments about the use of military force.

Given the present balance of strategic forces and the present state of nuclear technology, neither the East nor the West can achieve meaningful superiority if the other side is vigilant. The fact is that parity exists today. Maintaining that parity should be our goal for the future.

During a recent visit to the Soviet Union I was asked by several Russian political and scientific leaders to define nuclear parity. I replied that parity exists when each side is deterred from initiating a strategic strike by the recognition that such an attack would be followed by a retaliatory strike that would inflict unacceptable damage on the attacker. I went on to say: "I will surprise you by stating that I believe parity existed in October 1962, at the time of the Cuban missile crisis. The United States then had approximately five thousand strategic warheads, compared to the Soviet's three hundred. Despite an advantage of seventeen to one in our favor, President Kennedy and I were deterred from even considering a nuclear attack on the USSR by the knowledge that, although such a strike would destroy the Soviet Union, tens of their weapons would survive to be launched against the United States. These would kill millions of Americans. No responsible political leader would expose his nation to such a catastrophe."

One conclusion I draw from this story is that the "width" of the "band of parity" is very, very great. In 1962 it would have made no difference in our behavior whether the ratio had been seventeen to one, five to one, or two to one in our favor —or even two to one against us. In none of these cases would either we or the Soviets have felt we could use, or threaten to use, nuclear power to achieve a political end.

At today's force levels—when each side possesses ten or eleven thousand strategic warheads—the width of the band of parity is even greater than it was in 1962. In these circumstances it is inconceivable to me that either side "has superiority" or could move in ways that would permit it to achieve superiority. Parity is all we can hope for. And to maintain parity does not require that we match the other side weapon for weapon. Given that today the U.S. and Soviet strategic forces are severely asymmetrical—for example, we have far more of our strategic strength at sea than they do—an understanding and acceptance of the width of the band of parity gives much latitude in arms control negotiations for agreeing on reductions in force levels.

I should point to a second lesson that can be drawn from the Cuban experience. It is perhaps the most paradoxical tenet of the nuclear age. It was not enough that the United States was firmly deterred from initiating the use of nuclear weapons if the Soviets were uncertain of this fact. They were keenly aware of the seventeen-to-one advantage. It is probable that they feared the United States might try to use its numerical superiority. This Soviet insecurity put our country in great danger for one very simple reason: any indication that we were planning an attack would have placed severe pressures on Soviet leaders to launch a preemptive strike against us. If the Soviets had felt that a U.S. attack was imminent, they would have been tempted to move to destroy as large a portion of the American nuclear force as possible, rather than wait and allow its full strength of five thousand warheads to be launched against them.

It is very much in the interest of both sides to move away from such extremely unstable situations. They can do so by reducing the perceptions of vulnerability. To move in this direction is to increase what is called "crisis stability."

Severe crises have developed in the past between East and West. There is reason to believe they may in the future. Ensuring "crisis stability" should be a top priority in American force planning and arms control negotiations. The United States should pursue this objective both unilaterally and through agreement with the Soviet Union. Later in this book I will discuss concrete proposals for accomplishing this.

The concept of crisis stability may appear to be a contradictory one. It suggests that it is in the best interests of the United States to make its adversary feel more secure. Many argue precisely the opposite: it is important to keep the Soviet Union on the defensive and wary of American strength. But in the age of nuclear weapons, where one country holds the fate of another in its hands, old rules no longer apply. One story clearly illustrates this paradox.

In 1962 the columnist Stewart Alsop visited me in my Pentagon office. He had just learned, he said, that the CIA had evidence the Soviets were hardening their missile sites to make them more difficult to destroy. Wasn't I concerned? he asked. I said, "Stew, I never comment on information relating to the CIA. But let me say this: if the Soviets are hardening their missile sites, thank God." Alsop printed my views in the *Saturday Evening Post.* The Congress was outraged. Several congressmen literally asked for my resignation. What kind of Secretary of Defense, they asked, would be pleased that the Soviets were strengthening their forces?

My point was, of course, that the Soviets had only three hundred strategic warheads and their missiles and bombers were "soft," meaning they were vulnerable to attack. In a period of tension I wanted the Soviet leaders to have confidence that those forces would survive an American attack and would be capable of retaliating effectively. Then they would not feel a pressure to use them preemptively. I wanted to improve crisis stability. I had no desire to face, in a period of tension, an adversary who felt cornered, panicky, and desperate and who might be tempted to move irrationally. If the Soviets hardened their silos, and if this made them less fearful of a U.S. first strike, all the better for the United States.

Attempts to move away from parity toward superiority may look like policies of deterrence to one side, but they often appear to the other as support for a plan to fight and win a nuclear war. The fear, on our part, that the Soviets have, or are seeking to achieve, a first-strike capability is the next misperception I will address.

THE SOVIETS POSSESS A FIRST-STRIKE CAPABILITY

The arms race is driven by deep-seated fears on each side that the other has, or is seeking, the ability to execute a "first strike" —a strike that would effectively disarm the opponent and thereby force surrender.

The Committee on the Present Danger, a coalition of prominent individuals who opposed the SALT agreements, has stated, "By its continuing strategic nuclear buildup, the Soviet Union demonstrates that it does not subscribe to American notions of nuclear sufficiency and mutually assured deterrence." "Soviet nuclear and offensive and defensive forces," the committee has warned, "are designed to enable the USSR to fight, survive and win an all-out nuclear war." A report from the Office of the Secretary of Defense states that the deployment in "significant numbers" of Soviet SS-25 missiles (a newly developed mobile launcher carrying a highly accurate warhead) would "erode deterrence by allowing the Soviets to contemplate a first-strike using their fixed ICBMs, while retaining intact a reserve force of mobile missiles resistant to counter-attack." And President Reagan has emphasized his view:

> Everything that has been said, and everything in their manuals indicates that, unlike us, the Soviet Union believes that a nuclear war is possible. And they believe it's winnable, which means that they believe that if you could achieve enough superiority, then your opponent wouldn't have retaliatory strike capacity.

These statements make clear that the large force of powerful and increasingly accurate Soviet ICBMs has created the fear of a first strike in the minds of many U.S. leaders. According to this scenario,

> the Soviet missiles could, with one stroke, eliminate most of our Minuteman ICBMs; our surviving submarines and bombers would enable us only to retaliate against Soviet cities; but we would not do so because of our fear of a Soviet counterattack on our urban population; and thus

we would have no choice but to yield to all Soviet demands.

A more subtle variant of this "window of vulnerability" scenario would have the Soviets exacting political blackmail by merely threatening such an attack.

Those who accept the first-strike scenario view the Soviet ICBMs and the men who command them as objects in a universe decoupled from the real world.

They assume that Soviets leaders are confident that their highly complex systems, which have been tested only individually and in a controlled environment, would perform their myriad tasks in perfect harmony during the most cataclysmic battle in history; that our electronic eavesdropping satellites would detect no hint of the intricate preparations that such a strike would require; that we would not launch our missiles when the attack was detected; and that the thousands of American submarine-based and airborne warheads that would surely survive would not be used against a wide array of vulnerable Soviet military targets. Finally, they assume Soviet confidence that we would not use those vast surviving forces to retaliate against the Soviet population, even though tens of millions of Americans would have been killed as a result of the Soviet attack on our silos.

Only madmen would contemplate such a gamble. Whatever else they may be, the leaders of the Soviet Union are not madmen.

That a first strike is not a rational Soviet option has also been stated, as I indicated earlier, by President Reagan's own Scowcroft commission. That commission found that, under present circumstances, no combination of attacks from Soviet submarines and land-based ICBMs could catch our bombers on the ground as well as our Minutemen in their silos. In addition, our submarines at sea, which carry a substantial percentage of the U.S. strategic warheads, are safe from attack. In the race between techniques to hide submarines and those to find them, the fugitives have always been ahead and are widening their lead. As Vice Admiral Nils R. Thunman, the deputy chief of naval operations for submarine warfare, has said, there is "factual and authoritative assurance that there is no foreseeable technological capability by which the Soviets could significantly diminish the strategic effectiveness of the U.S. submarine missile force."

The Soviet leaders deny that they are seeking a first-strike capability. Brezhnev stated in 1977, for example, "The allegations that the Soviet Union is going beyond what is sufficient for defense, that it is striving for superiority in arms, with the aim of delivering a 'first strike,' are absurd and utterly unfounded."

The problem of arriving at a correct interpretation of Soviet strategy is compounded by the fact that the Soviets have reciprocal concerns about U.S. intentions. Their view of us is the mirror image of our view of them. Our deployment of the highly accurate MX missile, carrying ten warheads, in vulnerable Minuteman silos, they argue, can only be explained as part of a U.S. first-strike strategy. The MX, they have stated, is designed "not for deterrence but for launching a first strike and waging a nuclear war." Soviet statements on President Reagan's Star Wars proposal also make constant references to first-strike capabilities. Yuri Andropov stated in 1983, one week after President Reagan first proposed the Strategic Defense Initiative (SDI):

On the face of it, laymen may even find it attractive since the President speaks about what seem to be defensive measures. But this may seem to be so only on the face of it and only to those who are not conversant with these matters. In fact the strategic offensive forces of the United States will continue to be developed and upgraded at full tilt and along quite a definite line at that, namely that of acquiring a first nuclear strike capability.

Soviet fears of a U.S. first strike are unfounded. But they are understandable.

When I served in the Kennedy Administration, I learned that the capability to launch a first strike that would virtually eliminate Soviet nuclear forces was indeed the goal of some in the U.S. Air Force. In a 1962 memorandum to the President, I quoted from an Air Force document:

The Air Force has rather supported the development of forces which provide the United States a first-strike capability credible to the Soviet Union, as well as to our Allies, by virtue of our ability to limit damage to the United States and our Allies to levels acceptable in the light of the circumstances and the alternatives available.

I opposed the Air Force's recommendation. Kennedy accepted my judgment.

The United States does not now have the capability for a disarming first strike. No Administration has sought to achieve one at any time during the past quarter century. I am confident President Reagan is not seeking to do so today. But, given the composition of U.S. forces, the direction of our technology, and past statements like the one above, it is not surprising that such Soviet fears exist.

So I repeat: U.S. and USSR reciprocal fears of first-strike vulnerability persist. They are real. And, in a crisis, it matters what the other side believes—not what is objectively true. These fears are leading to the development of new weapons systems that each will view as highly threatening when the opponent also acquires them. Thus, our newest submarines will soon carry missiles accurate enough to destroy Soviet silos. When the Soviets follow suit, as they always do, their off-shore submarines will for the first time pose a simultaneous threat to our command centers, bomber bases, and Minuteman ICBMs.

The first-strike fears—real fears, though based on misperceptions—must be dealt with; I will have more to say on how to do so in Chapter 4.

THE SOVIETS EXPAND THEIR NUCLEAR FORCES NO MATTER WHAT WE DO

Many Americans are under the impression that while the United States expands its nuclear forces at some times, and shows restraint at others, the Soviet Union pursues a relentless, inexorable buildup. President Reagan, for example, has said: "We've tried time and time again to set an example by cutting our own forces in the hope that the Soviets would do likewise. The result has always been that they keep building." From this it is argued the United States must continue to expand merely to catch up.

The reality of the matter is much more complex than such misperceptions suggest. Soviet decisions about the forces that they will build are not simply the result of an internally motivated drive for power and superiority. Many of their force increases over the past twenty years can best be understood as reactions to American developments. In reverse, the same applies to many American developments. I have referred to this as the "action-reaction phenomenon." It is a fundamental force driving the nuclear arms race.

I do not mean to suggest that Soviet weapons programs can be explained as nothing more than direct reactions to U.S. programs. Clearly, they have pursued different paths, sought to exploit their own strengths, followed their own strategic thought, and dealt with distinct domestic pressures. Nonetheless, they have been strongly influenced by U.S. decisions and directions in the same way that their decisions have influenced us. The action-reaction phenomenon has contributed to the situation we face today. By understanding it we can limit its influence in the future. The following examples illustrate how it operates.

While serving as Secretary, I was repeatedly forced to make decisions about the forces we would begin to build today to balance Soviet forces that we believed might exist tomorrow. Such decisions were speculative, based on incomplete, often contradictory, and constantly changing information.

The production lead time on our force level increases was perhaps five years. Weapons development decisions often did not translate into operational forces in less than ten years. Therefore, when making production or development decisions, we were forced to guess what Soviet forces would look like five or ten years in the future. We had a limited knowledge of Soviet capabilities to develop and produce missiles and bombers—we had no information on how they intended to use those capabilities. As a result, we leaned toward worst-case assumptions. We assumed, in other words, the Soviets would maximize the use of their resources.

How did this affect the arms race?

Table 4 shows the results of thirty-five years of action and reaction. In 1960 and 1961 the United States had 68 missiles. The Soviets had a lesser number. We assumed they would build up rapidly. We therefore ordered several hundred Minuteman and Polaris missiles for delivery by 1965. We misjudged Soviet intentions. In 1965, therefore, our missile force carried 1,050 warheads compared to their 225. Between 1965 and 1970 we added only 750 warheads, the Soviets 1,375, nearly twice as many. But they were simply trying to catch up. They didn't make it. In 1970 our missile force carried 1,800 warheads, theirs 1,600.

TABLE 4. GROWTH OF U.S. AND SOVIET STRATEGIC NUCLEAR WARHEADS

	1950	1955	1960	1965	1970	1975	1980	1985
U.S.								
Missile warheads			68	1,050	1,800	6,100	7,300	7,900
Bombs	450	4,750	6,000	4,500	2,200	2,400	2,800	3,300
Total	450	4,750	6,068	5,550	4,000	8,500	10,100	11,200
Soviet								
Missile warheads			some	225	1,600	2,500	5,500	9,300
Bombs		20	300	375	200	300	500	600
Total		20	300	600	1,800	2,800	6,000	9,900

Perhaps the most dramatic example of the action-reaction phenomenon is the development and introduction of MIRVs (multiple independently targetable reentry vehicles). These are individual warheads that can be aimed at different targets but which can be clustered together and carried aloft in bunches of three, ten, or more, by one missile launcher. MIRVs were introduced into both the U.S. and Soviet forces in the 1970s. Their development led to a quadrupling of the number of missile warheads—a truly explosive development in the arms race.

How did this come about?

In the mid-1960s we had irrefutable evidence that the Soviets were deploying an antiballistic missile (ABM) system around Moscow—a system to defend their capital against our long-range missiles. We made the reasonable—but perhaps incorrect—assumption that they would deploy the system across the entire Soviet Union. Why would anyone put a system around one city and nowhere else? Were a nationwide Soviet ABM system to be put in place, it would require that we make major changes in our force levels.

The Congress believed that the proper response was for the United States to deploy its own countrywide ABM system. The Army had been working on such systems since the late 1950s, first the Nike Zeus and later the Nike X. In 1966, therefore, the Congress authorized and appropriated $167.9 million to start production of a Nike system (when fully deployed, the weapons would probably have cost $30 billion). President Johnson and I believed the system would provide little, if any, protection to either our population or to our weapons. We refused to spend the funds Congress had appropriated.

On December 6, 1966, Deputy Secretary of Defense Cyrus Vance, the Joint Chiefs of Staff, and I went to Austin, Texas, to meet with the President and Walt Rostow, special assistant to the President for national security affairs. Our purpose was to review with the President the defense budget for the fiscal year 1968, which was to be presented to the Congress in February 1967. Among the items to be considered was the recommendation of the chiefs that the budget request include funds for production of an antiballistic missile system. I explained to the President that the chiefs had recommended the action, but that Cy and I strongly opposed it.

The President called on each of the five chiefs in turn, and each one of them urged approval of the ABM program. Rostow sided with the chiefs. This was an extraordinarily difficult moment for the President. I never hesitated to disagree with a unanimous recommendation of the chiefs if I felt it was the wrong decision. In this case, however, Congress had already passed a law authorizing production of the system. To continue to refuse to proceed in the direction supported by the Congress, and to do so in the face of a unanimous recommendation by the chiefs, put the President in an almost untenable position.

At that point I said to the President: "The chiefs' recommendation is wrong; it's absolutely wrong. The proper response to a Soviet ABM system is not the deployment of an admittedly 'leaky' U.S. defense. The proper response is action which will ensure that we maintain our deterrent capability in the face of the Soviet defense. What the chiefs are recommending has nothing to do with maintaining that deterrent. If our deterrent force (our offensive missiles and bombers) was of the proper size before the Soviets deployed their defenses, it must now be expanded to ensure that the same number of weapons will land on Soviet targets, after taking account of the attrition the U.S. missile forces will suffer as they pass through the Soviet defenses. So for the United States to deploy an ABM defense is the wrong response to the Soviet action. But since we are in this bind, why don't we do this: put a small amount of money in the budget for ABM procurement, but state in the budget, and in my written report to the Congress, that none of those funds will be spent, and no decision will be made to deploy an ABM system, until after we make every possible effort to negotiate an agreement with the Soviets which will prohibit deployment of defenses by either side and will limit offensive forces as well."

The President seized on this proposal as a way out of a very difficult position.

I informed Dean Rusk, the Secretary of State, of the President's decision. He immediately approached the Soviets, seeking to initiate negotiation of an ABM treaty. They refused to participate even in preliminary discussions of such an agreement.

In June 1967 the Soviet Premier, Aleksei Kosygin, came to New York to visit the United Nations. After some difficulty, it was arranged for the Premier and President Johnson to meet on June 23 at Glassboro, New Jersey—Glassboro is halfway between New York and Washington—to discuss ABM deployment. At lunch that day the President, the Prime Minister, and a group of their associates were sitting around a small oval table. It was clear the President was becoming frustrated by Kosygin's failure to see the U.S. point of view on ABM defenses. Finally, the President turned to me and asked me to explain our position.

I said: "Mr. Prime Minister, you must understand that the proper U.S. response to your Soviet ABM system is an expansion of our offensive force. If we had the right number of offensive weapons to maintain a deterrent before you put your defenses in, then to maintain the same degree of deterrence, in the face of your defense, we must strengthen our offense. Deployment of a Soviet ABM system will lead to an escalation of the arms race. That's not good for either one of us."

Kosygin was furious. The blood rushed to his face, he pounded on the table, and he said, "Defense is moral; offense is immoral!" That was essentially the end of the discussion. The Soviet Union was by no means ready at that time to discuss an agreement banning defensive systems.

Following our return to Washington, there was unanimous agreement among the chiefs, the President, and me that we must initiate action to expand our offensive forces. The cheapest way to do that was to develop MIRVs. By placing more than one warhead on each missile, the United States could increase the number of warheads far more cheaply than by building more missiles. But we recognized this was a very dangerous step—if the Soviets followed our lead, as we must assume they would, it would lead to a dramatic increase in the offensive forces of each side. We therefore concluded that we would proceed with the development of MIRVs, but we would make no decision to deploy them until we had explored fully the possibilities of negotiating an agreement to prohibit defenses. If such a treaty was negotiated, the MIRV program would be scrapped.

When I left office in February 1968, the Soviets were still moving ahead with the ABM system and our MIRV program was acquiring a strong constituency in this country. What followed is a matter of record. The United States and the USSR did agree on an ABM Treaty in 1972, but it was decided, nonetheless, to proceed with deployment of MIRVs. U.S. missile warheads increased from 1,800 in 1970 to 6,100 in 1975; the Soviets, who were behind us in the development of MIRV technology, expanded their warheads by only 900 from 1,600 in 1970 to 2,500 in 1975.

The explosive growth in the number of Soviet missile warheads—which is pointed to by those who say "we build, they build; we stop, they build"—occurred between 1975 and 1980. During that period the Soviets more than doubled the number of their missile warheads, from 2,500 to 5,500. It was, in part, a delayed response to our MIRV decision of five years before. And it still left us in 1980 with a substantial numerical superiority: 7,300 to 5,500.

Since 1980 the Soviet buildup has continued. Today the number of warheads (missiles plus bombs) in the U.S. and Soviet strategic forces is approximately equal. But for thirty-five years, from 1950 to 1985, the Soviets lived with numerical inferiority, although, as I argued earlier, "parity" in operational terms has existed since at least October 1962.

It is essential to understand the action-reaction dynamic and to take it into account in formulating arms control and defense policies. We must learn to prepare for the bad without bringing on the worst. We must understand that every action stimulates a reaction in an endless cycle. Already the cost of our failure to do so has been the development of ridiculously large arsenals and missed opportunities to negotiate agreements to reduce them.

Some will argue that the action-reaction cycle can be broken if the West will take advantage of its lead in technology. This, too, is a misperception. I turn next to a discussion of this subject.

WE CAN BE TECHNOLOGICALLY SUPERIOR

The history of the arms race has been, in large part, the search by the West for a technological "fix" that will confer a lasting military advantage on it and reduce the power of the Soviet Union to threaten its security. In President Reagan's 1983 Star Wars speech, for example, he called on the scientific community, "who gave us nuclear weapons . . . to give us the means of rendering these nuclear weapons impotent and obsolete."

Americans place tremendous faith in technology. Not only President Reagan, but others as well, believe that it will allow us to escape the current nuclear stalemate. George Keyworth, former science advisor to the President, expressed that view: "We cannot look down each other's gun barrels indefinitely, regardless of the rational balance we think we can maintain. . . . Nor can we play into the Soviets' strong suit—men and materiel. Instead, we must start to play our trump—technological leverage." On another occasion Keyworth argued that "the Soviets have to play catch up when it comes to advanced technology. The U.S. should exploit this advantage by operating at the knowledge frontiers. In that way, by the expedient of always staying several steps ahead, we can thwart even the most aggressive attempts by adversaries to keep up."

Richard Wagner, assistant to the Secretary of Defense for atomic energy, asserts that technological superiority would bring important political advantages to the West:

I believe that our level of technology in itself, quite apart from exactly how it is built into fielded systems, affects [the Soviets'] overall image of themselves and of us, and thus can have a significant deterrent effect. . . . By the 1990s we'll need some really new technology to keep the image ratio in our favor.

As a result of these attitudes, the United States has repeatedly gone forward with advancements in nuclear weaponry. It has often led in the technology race, but the U.S. advantage has

TABLE 5. THE TECHNOLOGY RACE

Weapon	Date of Testing or Deployment	
	U.S.	Soviet
Atomic bomb	1945	1949
Intercontinental bomber	1948	1955
Jet bomber	1951	1954
Hydrogen bomb	1952	1953
ICBM	1958	1957
Satellite photoreconnaissance	1960	1962
Sub-launched Missile	1960	1964
Solid-fueled ICBM	1962	1966
ABM	1974	1966
Antisatellite Weapons	1963	1968
MIRV	1970	1975

been temporary. As Table 5 indicates, the U.S. innovations have been matched quickly by the Soviet Union and the arms race has escalated to yet a higher level.

Not only has the U.S. lead quickly evaporated in each instance, but several of the U.S. advances have, if anything, worked to the advantage of the Soviet Union. Three clear examples are MIRVs, sea-launched missiles, and antisatellite weapons. The attainment of these capabilities by each side has produced, or will produce, a net disadvantage for the United States.

As I said earlier, MIRVs were viewed as a relatively inexpensive way to expand U.S. offensive forces. However, historically, the Soviet Union, because it was less advanced in miniaturization than the United States, has relied upon larger missiles with more powerful boosters. This gave it a capability to mount on each missile launcher a larger number of MIRVs. Thus, MIRVing by both sides multiplied the Soviet forces by a larger factor.

The introduction of sea-launched missiles (both ballistic missiles and cruise missiles) by the United States, when fully matched by the Soviets, is also likely to lead to a Soviet advantage. The missiles present a greater threat to the United States because of our long and exposed coastline. Highly accurate ballistic missiles launched from Soviet submarines off U.S. shores will present a serious threat to our hardened targets (missile silos and command centers). Cruise missiles, also to be launched from submarines, are slow-moving, but very difficult to detect. Both they and the sea-launched ballistic missiles present a short-warning threat to our bomber bases.

Antisatellite weapons are a further example of a U.S. innovation that ultimately may be more threatening to the United States than to the Soviet Union. Antisatellite weapons are designed to attack and destroy satellites in space. The United States relies on its satellites for information, surveillance, and communications far more than does the Soviet Union. As a result, the United States would be at a greater disadvantage if each side were to deploy antisatellite systems. It would be very much in our interest to negotiate an arms control agreement that would prohibit further testing and deployment of these weapons.

Americans have a justified pride in their technological leadership. But in the area of nuclear weapons that pride must be tempered by a recognition of Soviet determination to match U.S. advances. As W. Averell Harriman, former ambassador to the Soviet Union, stated in 1982:

> My reading of the Soviet experience—and I have met with every Soviet leader from Stalin to Brezhnev—indicates that Moscow will make whatever sacrifice it takes to remain equal—as we will too. The conclusion will not be superiority; the end will be an arms race without end.

The long-term goal of U.S. policy should not be to achieve superiority in the arms race by adding numbers or sophistication, but rather to control and limit nuclear arms competition through formal and informal agreements. I will turn next to the discussion of several misperceptions which stand in the way of achieving that objective.

THE NUCLEAR BUILDUP WAS INEVITABLE

Some have suggested that arms control is fundamentally inconsistent with the East-West rivalry, that mutual fear and distrust will inevitably rule out steps to control the arms race, that as long as we are adversaries we cannot cooperate in significant ways. Some look at the last fifty years and draw the lesson that slowing the nuclear arms race is a herculean task and reversing it an impossible one. I draw a different lesson. I look at the past half century and see fifty years of missed opportunities.

There is one central mind-set that has repeatedly prevented us from agreeing to limit the advance of nuclear technology and the production of nuclear weapons. We consistently tend to exaggerate the risks associated with an agreement, while failing to recognize the consequences of proceeding with no constraints. It is correct to point out that every attempt to control the arms race is likely to carry risk with it. But it is equally correct to emphasize that failure to accept mutual restraints often carries risk as well.

The risks of an unrestrained arms race are growing. Guidance systems are becoming more accurate and thus more threatening to the opponent. Continuing miniaturization is enhancing mobility. The result will be increasingly lethal systems that are more and more difficult to detect.

There are very real risks in the continued modernization of nuclear arsenals. These must be balanced against the risks of any agreement. Let me give just two examples of important opportunities forgone because we failed to make such judgments: the opportunity to negotiate a comprehensive test ban in 1963, and the opportunity to prohibit deployment of MIRVs in 1972.

In August 1963 the Kennedy Administration negotiated the Limited Test Ban Treaty. That treaty banned nuclear testing in the atmosphere but permitted testing to continue underground. The reason the Administration did not seek a complete ban on testing was not, as some have suggested, because it could not have been negotiated or adequately verified. Rather, it was President Kennedy's view, a view shared by

Secretary Rusk and myself, that a comprehensive test ban (CTB) treaty would not have been ratified by two-thirds of the Senate. In fact, the Limited Test Ban Treaty was passed by the Senate only because of several important conditions that were attached to it. These included a requirement that the United States would pursue a vigorous testing program underground and expensive preparations for resumption of atmospheric testing to guarantee that we would be ready to respond quickly to Soviet violations of the ban.

Reluctantly, the Chiefs of Staff, to the great surprise of the Senate, testified in support of the Limited Test Ban. Neither the chiefs nor the Senate were prepared to take the additional step of moving to a comprehensive ban. They both believed the Soviet Union might violate the ban without the knowledge of the United States. They feared the USSR might achieve some significant military advantage through such violations.

But I am confident that a pattern of Soviet violations could not have proceeded for long without our knowledge. And if we look back at that decision today, we can see clearly the costs of not going forward with the comprehensive test ban. As I have said, in the early 1960s the United States had some 5,000 strategic warheads and the Soviet Union had roughly 300. In addition, the United States had an enormous lead over the Soviets in every aspect of nuclear weapons technology. At that time we had completed 293 nuclear tests compared to the Soviets' 130. What knowledgeable expert would deny that, if we had frozen the technological competition at the level of the early sixties, the United States would be in a better position today?

With hindsight, it is clear there were tremendous costs to continued testing that were not properly considered in 1963.

The same can be said of the decision in 1972 to go ahead

with the deployment of MIRVs after the ABM Treaty had removed the initial justification for the program.

There were indications that the Soviets would have been willing in the early 1970s to negotiate a ban on MIRVs. Without doubt this would have led to smaller, less threatening nuclear forces than those in existence today. The story of why neither party pursued a MIRV ban is interesting.

As I discussed earlier, when MIRV "development" was authorized in the mid-1960s, it was an insurance program to counter what we feared would be a widespread deployment of the Soviet ABM system. When that threat failed to materialize, and particularly when U.S.-Soviet SALT negotiations began in the early 1970s, there was a real opportunity to terminate the programs.

There were clear incentives for both sides to prevent the full application of MIRV technology. The Soviets at that time were still in the early stages of developing a MIRV capability. The MIRVing of American forces would permit a tremendous expansion that the Soviets would be unable to match for a period of years. From the American perspective, the lead the United States held at that time in MIRV technology was clearly a temporary one. Without negotiated constraints on the application of MIRV technology, the Soviets surely would use it to multiply their forces and nullify American force increases.

During the SALT I negotiations, both the United States and the Soviet Union tabled proposals to limit MIRVs. Publicly, each blamed the other for failure to achieve a ban. In fact, neither the United States nor the Soviet Union expressed great disappointment over failure to limit MIRVs in the SALT I negotiations. At that time the United States was more concerned with exploiting its lead in MIRV technology and the Soviet Union in closing that lead. The United States was deploying MIRVed missiles during the negotiations, while the Soviet Union had not even begun to test them. American leaders were unwilling to negotiate away this advantage, regardless of Soviet concessions in return. Soviet leaders, for their part, were not willing to stop development of an important system that the United States currently monopolized.

Ambassador Gerard Smith, head of the U.S. SALT I delegation, in arguing the case for a MIRV ban to President Nixon in 1970, stated, "There would be risks in such a controlled environment but I believe that they are calculable, insurable . . . and reasonable ones to run." Tragically, the risks of forgoing MIRV technology appeared more pressing and persuasive to both sides than the less immediate but more significant risks of going forward. When asked in 1974 about the effort to limit MIRVs, former Secretary of State Henry Kissinger stated, "I would say in retrospect that I wish I had thought through the implications of a MIRVed world more thoughtfully in 1969 and in 1970 than I did."

The irony is that today we are approaching full circle. The Scowcroft commission has now called for a shift away from MIRVs and back to single-warhead missiles. The development of just such a weapon, the Midgetman, is now underway.

There have been other missed opportunities. In 1946, for example, while the United States still possessed a monopoly on nuclear weapons, it proposed creating an international agency that would take control of all nuclear weapons and material, after which the United States would relinquish its arsenal. The Soviets made a counterproposal without provisions for inspection or enforcement, and the two countries failed to reach a compromise between the two proposals. Since that time, of course, the number of nuclear warheads on both sides has increased to over fifty thousand.

Similar opportunities to slow, or reverse, the arms race exist today and will arise in the future. As we evaluate them, we must consider the risks of proceeding without restraint versus the risks, including the risk of possible violations, of limits both on technological advance and force level expansion.

THE SOVIETS CHEAT, SO AGREEMENTS ARE WORTHLESS

Dealing with the Soviets is a daunting prospect for many Americans. Clearly, the two countries share a common interest in avoiding nuclear war, and agreements that accomplish that will increase our security. Nonetheless, Americans are extremely wary and distrustful of Soviet motives.

Attacks on arms control generally play off this fear of the Soviet Union. Despite a strong commitment among most Americans to arms restraint, it will always be easy for America's skeptics to "play the Soviet card." One of the accusations they make most often is that the Soviets are cheating on their arms control treaties.

A very vocal and effective proponent of this line of argument is Richard Perle, assistant secretary of defense for international security policy. Perle claims that the Soviet Union has violated "almost all" of the most important arms control agreements signed since 1963. He warns, "To believe in far-reaching arms control with the Soviet Union in an adversarial position, you have to believe they'll change, change fundamentally, by reducing the prominence of military forces as a factor." And he concludes by saying, "The sense that we and the Russians could compose our differences, reduce them to treaty constraints, enter into agreements, treaties, reflecting a set of constraints and then rely on compliance to produce a safer world—I don't agree with any of that."

Specific Soviet actions cited by the Administration as violations include testing of a second "new type" of ICBM, the SS-25; excessive encoding of missile test data to impede verification; and construction of a radar near Krasnoyarsk. The first two actions are claimed to be violations of the SALT II Treaty and the third, with apparent justification, is said to be prohibited by the ABM Treaty. None of these pose serious threats to our security. Nonetheless, they all should be pursued forcefully through the proper channels. We have not done so.

The process of arms control does not require that we trust the Russians. As former SALT negotiator Paul Warnke explained: "If you figure you can't have arms control unless the Russians are nice guys, then it seems to me that you're being totally illogical. If the Russians could be trusted to be nice guys, you wouldn't need strategic arms control. And you wouldn't need strategic arms." I agree with Warnke. We need not trust the Russians other than to act in their own self-interest. If arms control agreements are not in the nature of plus-sum games— that is, if they are not in the interest of both parties—they should not be entered into.

I would go further and say the only arms control agreements in the interest of this country are agreements that the United States can verify by itself, without relying on the good faith of any other nation. An effective verification system is one that will detect, with a high degree of confidence, any set of violations having a significant impact on the strategic balance. Both the United States and the Soviet Union have this capacity.

The Soviet record of adherence to arms agreements is not as dim as many paint it. In 1985 Lieutenant General John Chain, then director of the Politico-Military Affairs Bureau at the State Department, testified before the Senate Armed Services Committee:

I believe that . . . if you take the body of the treaties in a macrosense, they [the Soviets] have complied with the large majority of the treaties. . . . I would hate to see this body walk out of here at the end of the day thinking of arms control as no good because the Soviets always cheat. That is not the position of the Administration. It certainly is not the position of the State Department.

President Reagan has expressed deep concern about possible Soviet violations of SALT II. But even after his May 27, 1986, "repudiation" of the agreement, he has continued with the U.S. policy of not undercutting the force limits specified in the treaty. He has done so, I believe, because the record is clear: when required by existing treaties' constraints, the Soviets have dismantled submarines, missile launchers, and bombers.*

Questions of compliance are rarely, if ever, black and white. As Secretary Weinberger stated in 1983, "Compliance issues are always very difficult, in part because existing agreements often contain vague or equivocal language of which there can be, in the nature of the case, no authoritative interpretation." Thus, it is very difficult to determine how to respond to those actions that seem to violate agreements but that have little or no military significance. It was precisely for this reason that the United States and the USSR established the Standing Consultative Commission (SCC) in 1972.

The SCC is the sole forum for discussion and resolution of SALT compliance questions. It has been used successfully in

---

*From 1972 to 1985, for example, the Soviet Union removed 1,007 land-based missiles and 233 submarine-based ballistic missiles from their active force and dismantled 13 Yankee-class ballistic-missile-carrying submarines as new weapons entered the force. On the U.S. side, 320 land-based and 544 submarine-based missiles have been removed and 11 ballistic-missile-carrying submarines dismantled.

settling both American and Soviet concerns and clarifying treaty provisions.

According to a joint paper of the State Department, the Defense Department, and the Arms Control and Disarmament Agency, issued during the Carter Administration:

> Soviet compliance under fourteen arms control agreements signed since 1959 has been good. We raised a number of issues with the Soviets in SALT I—as they did with us—but in every case the activity in question either ceased or subsequent information clarified the situation and allayed our concern.

What is considered one of the clearest violations of SALT —the construction of large shelters over missile silos—was committed by the United States. Through the SCC the Soviets raised concerns about the shelters, arguing they constituted deliberate concealment in violation of SALT I. In June 1979, with the signing of the SALT II Treaty, which specifically banned the use of such shelters, the United States stopped using them. The SCC has resolved some thirteen other issues raised by either the U.S. or the Soviet Union.

Despite this record, the Reagan Administration has placed little faith in the SCC. In a 1985 report to the President, the Pentagon characterized the SCC as "an Orwellian memory-hold into which our concerns have been dumped like yesterday's trash." It claimed that the SCC has failed to resolve "any significant compliance issue" in the thirteen years of its existence. The Administration has taken many of its allegations, including the three I mentioned earlier in this section, directly to the public without using the SCC process to the fullest extent possible.

In response to alleged Soviet violations of SALT II, the Administration has announced a policy of "proportionate responses," reserving the right to commit violations of the treaty to match Soviet violations. Specifically, it has suggested the United States might go forward with testing and deployment of the Midgetman, clearly prohibited by the treaty, in response to Soviet deployment of the SS-25. Given Soviet insistence that they are in compliance with SALT II, such a move by the United States would invite similar Soviet responses and the rapid erosion of the treaty. This is a shortsighted way to pursue compliance questions and would undermine confidence in the entire arms control regime. The second report of the Scowcroft commission described the difficulty of responding firmly but constructively to violations of marginal military significance:

> Even though they may not have significant military impact, such violations erode the confidence of the American people and government in the agreements themselves. In addition, failure to take action may encourage the Soviets to believe they can act with impunity. There may not always be available, however, effective responses proportionate to the violations themselves. The proper course of action is to maintain a system of communication for review and correction of such incidents.

The agreed-upon system of communication is the Standing Consultative Commission. We should use it fully. The record clearly shows that if both sides make full use of the committee process, compliance with arms treaties can be achieved.

AGREEMENTS HAVE ONLY LET
THE SOVIETS GET AHEAD

A third misperception associated with the arms control process
is that not only do the Soviets cheat on their bargains, but the
bargains themselves were written to favor the Soviet Union.
This charge is leveled most often against the SALT II Treaty.
According to Secretary Weinberger:

> In no area have we ignored reality so long as in our effort
> to negotiate and enforce arms control. . . . We did succeed
> in restraining our own strategic programs, but certain-
> ly not those of the Soviet Union. The SALT I accord
> . . . did not significantly impede the growth of the strate-
> gic offensive capacity of the Soviet Union; as for SALT
> II, had you [the Senate] ratified it in the form proposed,
> that treaty would have permitted an enormous further
> increase in Soviet offensive capacity, while presenting the
> danger of lulling us into a false sense of security.

"There is nothing in SALT II," claims Richard Perle, "that is
important for our security."

The President has expressed the same view as Perle. Mr.
Reagan asserted during his first presidential campaign:

> The SALT II Treaty was the result of negotiations that
> Mr. Carter's team entered into after he had asked the
> Soviet Union for a discussion of actual reduction of nu-
> clear strategic weapons, and his emissary . . . came home
> in 12 hours having heard a very definite "nyet." . . . We
> then went back into negotiations on their terms, because
> Mr. Carter had cancelled the B-1 bomber, delayed the

MX, delayed the Trident submarine, delayed the cruise missile, shut down the Minuteman missile production line, and whatever other things that might have been done. The Soviet Union sat at the table knowing that we had gone forward with unilateral concessions without any reciprocation from them whatsoever.

The central elements of the Reagan Administration's strategic modernization program were, in fact, initiated by the previous administrations—those of Nixon, Ford, and Carter. But more to the point, although the SALT II Treaty negotiated during that time did permit the expansion of Soviet forces, the treaty did not cause it. Furthermore, without the constraints imposed on both sides, current force levels almost certainly would have been higher.

As I described earlier in this chapter, the Soviet Union did expand the number of its strategic warheads under the SALT II Treaty. When the negotiations officially began in 1972, the Soviet Union had some eighteen hundred warheads and the United States four thousand. The Soviets clearly would not agree to a document that froze them into a posture of numerical inferiority. So when the United States insisted on limits high enough to accommodate our MIRV programs, they clearly left room for substantial Soviet expansion. The result is that today each side has about eleven thousand warheads. Under the treaty each side can (and probably will) expand its force to a total of approximately thirteen thousand.

Criticisms of SALT II ignore, as Appendix IV indicates, that Soviet expansion would probably have been even greater without the treaties in place. Once again, this demonstrates the mind-set that sees the risks of an agreement but fails to balance those against the costs of no agreement whatsoever. The most valid criticism that can be made about past strategic

offensive agreements is that they have only modestly constrained both sides. The record of arms control merely shows
that we need much more of it.

NUCLEAR WEAPONS, EVEN WHEN
MILITARILY IRRELEVANT, CAN
SERVE POLITICAL ENDS

The arms race is fueled in part by the creation of political
myths around military hardware. Frequently, nuclear systems,
which serve no military purpose, are deployed to send political
signals—signals of "reassurance" to U.S. allies and "resolve" to
the Soviet Union.

One recent example of such an action has been the installa-
tion of the Pershing II and cruise missiles in Europe. An
ex-Prime Minister of a major European nation admitted to me
that the weapons are militarily irrelevant. He stressed, however, that they are needed to strengthen the political perception that the United States would come to the defense of
Europe if the Soviets attacked. His reasoning was as follows:

- It is correct to say that the Soviet targets covered by the
  American missiles from their bases in Europe could be
  attacked equally well by existing Polaris or Minuteman
  forces.
- However, the European people question whether an
  American President would authorize launch of the Polaris or Minuteman in response to an attack on Europe by
  the Soviet intermediate-range SS-20 missiles. They believe the President would hold back for fear that the
  launch of the Polaris and Minutemen would draw a
  Soviet attack on the United States.
- Therefore, to convince the Europeans that an SS-20

attack will lead to an American response—and hence to give them confidence in NATO's ability to deter such an attack—it is necessary to base the American missiles on the soil of Europe.

The fallacy of the argument lies in the fact that in either case the decision to use the U.S. forces must be made by the President. And the same factors that would influence his decision to launch missiles based in the United States against Russian targets would determine whether he would authorize attacks from European bases. The President would recognize that from Moscow's perspective it would make no difference if the American nuclear weapons that hit Soviet targets were launched from a U.S. submarine or from U.S. forces in Germany. The probable response in either case would be retaliation against the United States.

A U.S. President is no more or less likely to authorize the use of European-based forces against Soviet targets than he is to authorize the use of U.S.-based systems.

So the idea that the Pershing and cruise missiles are necessary as a counter to Soviet forces is a myth. Because the basing of these weapons in Europe has come to be seen by many Europeans as a test of Alliance resolve and a visible symbol of the American nuclear commitments, the misperception must be treated as reality. But surely we have not become so sanguine about the risks of the arms race that we can afford to convey political signals with weapons of mass destruction.

The arms race in the first half century of the nuclear age has been fueled in part by myths such as the ones I have described. If we continue on this path for another fifty years, we will be led not only to further increases in the numbers of weapons, but to greater danger of their use in time of tension. In the next chapter, I will consider alternatives to this prospect.

4.

THE NEXT HALF CENTURY

Alternative Ways of
Reducing the Risk
of Nuclear War,
1990–2040

The absurd struggle to improve the ability to wage nuclear war has shaken confidence in our ability to avert that war. The conviction that we must change course is shared by groups and individuals as diverse as the freeze movement, the President, the Catholic and Methodist bishops, the majority of the nation's top scientists, Soviet leader Mikhail Gorbachev, and such leaders of Third World and independent nations as Rajiv Gandhi and the late Olof Palme. All agree that we need a plan to reduce the long-term risk of nuclear war, but there is no consensus on what course to take. The changes of direction being advocated follow from very different diagnoses of our predicament.

Before examining proposals for changing course, it should be emphasized that if the superpowers continue to weaken the arms control regime, as they have over the past six or seven years, the risk of the world ultimately facing a nuclear conflagration will continue to grow. We are on the verge of a dramatic escalation of the arms race—an escalation to levels that will be more and more difficult, if not impossible, to control.

Miniaturization is increasing the mobility, accuracy, and destructive power of weapons. In advanced stages of development are mobile land-based missiles; antisatellite weapons; space-based systems; and land-, sea-, and air-based cruise missiles that are increasingly difficult to detect and hence increasingly difficult to limit by verifiable arms control agreements.

Our current nuclear-weapons-building program, which is

producing two thousand warheads annually, is the biggest in twenty years. And steps are underway to expand substantially, for the 1990s, both the production of the key nuclear materials —tritium, uranium, and plutonium—and the production of the warheads themselves. At the same time, our weapons laboratories are forecasting large increases in the number of underground tests required for the development of new types of nuclear arms. Officials at the Los Alamos Scientific Laboratory said recently that although in the past only about six nuclear tests were required to develop a weapon, perfecting one of the new, more complex designs we are working on today will require at least one hundred to two hundred explosions. They say, "The physics processes we are looking at are far more complicated than anything we've looked at before."

Unconstrained weapons development and deployment over the next fifty years will lead not only to increased numbers of weapons but to greater danger of their use in time of tension, i.e., greater "crisis instability."

It is the recognition of this danger that has led the bishops, the President, the General Secretary, and others to suggest actions that they hope will reduce the long-term risk of nuclear war. The proposals they have presented include:

- Achieving political reconciliation between East and West.
- Eliminating all nuclear weapons through negotiation (as proposed by General Secretary Gorbachev).
- Replacing "deterrence" with "defense"—the elimination of nuclear weapons by the *substitution* of defensive forces for offensive forces (as proposed by President Reagan).
- Strengthening deterrence by *adding* defensive forces to the offense (as proposed by Henry Kissinger).

• Accepting the proposition that nuclear warheads have no military use whatsoever except to deter one's opponent's use of such weapons. Such a view would require fundamental adjustments in NATO's strategy, war plans, and conventional force levels; weapons development programs; and arms control agreements.

Do any of these alternatives offer hope that the second half of the first century of the nuclear age will differ from the first?

EAST-WEST RECONCILIATION

The East-West military rivalry is, of course, a function of the political conflict that divides the two blocs. Many have argued, therefore, that any long-term attempt to bring a halt to the arms race and to reduce the risk of nuclear war must begin by addressing the source of the tensions—the political rivalry.

Two years ago an international panel, of which I was a member, addressed this issue. The group included six former Prime Ministers, three former Foreign Ministers, two former Defense Ministers, and more than twenty other leading diplomats, businessmen, and scholars from ten Western countries. Because of the experience of the participants, the breadth of the research program, and the extent of the consultative process, the panel's report is, I believe, a definitive statement of the nature of the problem and alternative approaches to its solution. I will draw freely upon it in commenting upon the possibility of political reconciliation.

I begin by stressing my conviction that North America, Western Europe, and Japan lack an agreed conceptual framework for the management of relations with the Soviet Union and its allies. No serious or thoughtful person can possibly be happy with the current state of those relations. Although in recent months we have seen the beginnings of long-overdue discussions of both the military and political aspects of the relationship, we should not delude ourselves about the substantial impediments to an amelioration of the underlying conflict.

The last five years of basically routine and institutionalized hostility have been enormously damaging to the fabric of the relationship. They have served to produce an atmosphere in which contacts between East and West have been severely reduced, mistrust has deepened, thinking has become excessively militarized, and the risks of dangerous misunderstandings have grown. The problem has been compounded by both sides' reckless acquisition of ever more sophisticated and expensive weapons which themselves engender additional tensions and impose immense economic costs threatening serious damage to our economic systems.

We in the West need a coherent, widely supported policy, rooted in reality and pressed with conviction and determination. It must be a policy which protects vital interests, enhances political cohesion, and offers the hope of influencing Soviet policy in a favorable direction. A long-term, stable relationship between East and West is both desirable and attainable. Even in an atmosphere of competition and mutual suspicion there are common interests, and the pursuit of each side's competitive goals can take place in an atmosphere of moderation.

Development of such an understanding with the Soviet Union and its allies will not come easily. No illusion should be harbored about the nature of the Soviet system, about its hostility to Western values and aspirations, nor about the speed with which the two systems will converge. For traditional Marxists, the Soviet system is not only a country, but a cause, based on the proposition that our system will disappear. But we cannot permit ourselves the mirror image of that proposition; the Soviets will not disappear. History teaches us that even enduring enmities between states or groups of states can take second place to specific interests. Both sides share the imperative of the survival of their respective societies. Compromises are not only possible; in the final analysis, they are the only alternative to disaster.

The Western objectives, therefore, can best be served through a process of "sustained engagement" that will increase markedly all areas of contact with the East. Our agenda should be far more comprehensive than hitherto attempted. Narrow approaches focusing primarily on one or another functional aspects of the relationship—for example, arms control—are not enough. The dialogue needs to be broad-based, multi-faceted, and continuous.

Political relations between East and West will have to be substantially improved and intensified if other changes are to be affected and sustained. Recent history has vividly illuminated that without an improved political climate, functional agreements are unlikely to be effective.

The political relationship must rest on the twin pillars of firmness and flexibility. It is abundantly clear that both of these elements are essential if our policies are to command public support and have a chance of succeeding. There is not a contradiction here: détente without defense would amount to surrender on the installment plan; defense without détente would increase tensions and the risk of conflict. The two are mutually reinforcing.

When one turns from political relationships to matters of trade and finance, there are even greater voids to bridge. The U.S. has had no consistent trade policy with the USSR. In recent years we have been responsible on several occasions for self-inflicted wounds over the question of the efficacy and employment of economic sanctions vis-à-vis the Eastern bloc.

We need to recognize from the outset that trade is advantageous to both sides, not a favor which the West grants to the East or a reward for good conduct. And we must rid ourselves of the idea that the Soviet economy may "collapse" and of the equally farfetched notion that the West has either the power or the duty to contribute in a significant way to the collapse or the reform of that enormous machine. The dreams harbored by some in the West that the withholding of trade will intensify Eastern difficulties and bring about systemic changes are simply not realistic. But they are, I would argue, dangerous and politically very damaging.

The relationships between Eastern and Western governments—contacts at the official level—are of course fundamental. But we should not neglect the need to further develop relations between the peoples of East and West in such areas as science, the arts and humanities, and education. A high priority should be given to dispelling the ignorance and misunderstanding each side has of the other. This task by its nature involves more than governments.

In sum, we are, I believe, at a crucial juncture in East-West relations, a point at which fundamental choices need to be made by our governments and our peoples about the type of relationship we desire with the Soviet Union and its allies. They are immensely important choices, which will have reverberations for years to come.

I, along with those who participated with me in preparing the report *Managing East-West Conflict*, strongly urge that we embark upon a program of "sustained engagement." It cannot be stressed enough, however, that this process will require time, patience, and consistency of purpose. And there are limits to the results. It cannot be expected to eliminate the periods of tension and confrontation that have characterized East-West relations over the past four decades. It is not, therefore, a substitute for other actions designed to reduce the risk that military conflict, rising out of such confrontation, will lead to the use of nuclear weapons. Steps to control and reverse the arms race must go forward in parallel with efforts to reduce political tension.

George Kennan, one of our nation's foremost Soviet experts, has stressed this point. He has repeatedly warned that the nuclear arms race, like so many previous arms races, has taken on a momentum and pace of its own, apart from the context of the political relationship which gave rise to it. In 1981, upon receiving the Albert Einstein Peace Prize, he said:

> This [the arms race] is nothing new. I am a diplomatic historian. I see this same phenomenon playing its fateful part in the relations among the great European powers as much as a century ago. I see this competitive buildup of armaments conceived initially as a means to an end but soon becoming the end itself. I see it taking possession of men's imagination and behavior, becoming a force in its own right, detaching itself from the political differences that initially inspired it, and then leading both parties, invariably and inexorably, to the war they no longer know how to avoid.

This dynamic must be addressed directly. The urgency of the nuclear problem and the clear common interest in reducing the risk of nuclear war offer unprecedented incentives to the East and the West to seek arms control agreements despite the political barriers of mistrust and suspicion that divide them. Again, according to Kennan:

> Adequate words are lacking to express the full seriousness of our present situation. It is not just that we are for the

moment on a collision course politically with the Soviet Union, and that the process of rational communication between the two governments seems to have broken down completely; it is also—and even more importantly—the fact that the ultimate sanction behind the conflicting policies of these two governments is a type and volume of weaponry which could not possibly be used without utter disaster for us all.

I turn next to the consideration of four different approaches to controlling directly the "volume" and "use" of such weaponry.

GORBACHEV: ELIMINATE ALL NUCLEAR WEAPONS

Mikhail Gorbachev, General Secretary of the Soviet Communist Party, has proposed that the United States and the Soviet Union begin a phased transition aimed at achieving the total elimination of nuclear weapons by the year 2000. Although in the early 1960s President Kennedy and the then Soviet General Secretary Nikita Khrushchev traded proposals for "general and complete disarmament," Gorbachev's dramatic proposal has reopened the debate on the desirability and feasibility of complete destruction of the world's nuclear arsenals.

Is a nuclear-free world desirable? I believe it is, and I think most Americans would agree. In his second inaugural address President Reagan said, "We seek the total elimination one day of nuclear weapons from the face of the Earth." President Carter, in his inaugural address, endorsed the same goal.

However, as I noted in Chapter 2, NATO's current military strategy and war plans are based on the opposite premise. And many—I would say most—U.S. military and civilian officials, as well as European leaders, hold the view that nuclear weapons are a necessary deterrent to Soviet aggression with conventional forces. Thus, these individuals do not favor a world without nuclear weapons. Zbigniew Brzezinski, President Carter's national security advisor, said of Gorbachev's proposal, "It is a plan for making the world safe for conventional warfare. I am therefore not enthusiastic about it." Other Western officials have responded to Gorbachev by suggesting that nuclear disarmament would not be desirable without dramatic changes in the superpower relationship, including the correction of the conventional-force imbalances, full compliance with existing and future treaty obligations, peaceful resolution of regional conflicts in ways that allow free choice without outside interference, and a demonstrated commitment by the Soviet Union to peaceful competition throughout the world.

My criticism of Gorbachev's vision, however, is not that it is undesirable, but that it is infeasible under foreseeable circumstances. Indeed, an agreement to eliminate all nuclear weapons, given political and technical realities, could, paradoxically, increase the risk of nuclear war. Why? Because even if distrust between the superpowers could be substantially reduced, the fear of cheating on such an agreement would be very great indeed.

Policing an arms control agreement that restricted each side to a small number of nuclear weapons—say a few hundred—is feasible. Either side might be able to engage in some marginal cheating by building a small number of additional warheads, but such cheating would not alter the condition of mutual parity in nuclear forces. If cheating took place on a scale sufficient to upset the balance—if, for example, one side began a building and testing project aimed at deploying a new generation of weaponry—the other side would certainly detect that activity in time to take corresponding actions to maintain parity. Thus, neither small- nor large-scale cheating could secure a strategic advantage, and both sides would have little incentive to try to "break out" of the agreement.

The situation would be quite different in a nuclear-free world. The difficulties of designing an agreement to eliminate all nuclear weapons and to ensure strategic stability during the period in which the superpowers and other nuclear states reduced their forces to zero would be substantial. Although we might be able to verify the dismantling of Soviet nuclear weapons, we could not cleanse the minds of U.S. and Soviet scientists of the knowledge of how to build them. Warheads might be eliminated, but the potential for recreating them would remain. And in a "nuclear-free world" a single nuclear weapon, the production and storage of which would be impossible to detect, could alter the military balance. We would live with the fear of waking up one day to find Mr. Gorbachev brandishing the world's only nuclear warhead, threatening to blackmail us into accepting his political demands.

Thus, we would have a strong incentive to secretly stockpile some nuclear bombs to protect ourselves against such a threat. The Soviets would harbor the same fears and would take the same kind of actions. These incentives would be reinforced by fears that a third country—perhaps one led by an unstable or fanatical leader—or even a terrorist group, might get hold of a bomb and challenge the superpowers for world influence. Sooner or later, one side would observe suspicious actions by the other and would take steps to protect itself by moving closer to actual deployment of nuclear weapons.

The small nuclear arsenals that could emerge under this scenario would be tempting targets in a crisis. Each side would have a strong incentive to launch a strike against the opponent's nuclear force or suspected nuclear facilities. In other words, crisis stability would be extremely low, and any conflict could quickly become a nuclear one. The prospect of global annihilation posed by arsenals of hundreds or thousands of nuclear weapons might be eliminated, but the likelihood of the use of some nuclear weapons could be substantially increased. And a single nuclear weapon could kill millions of people.

Unless we can develop technologies and procedures to ensure detection of any steps toward building a single nuclear bomb by any nation or terrorist group, an agreement for total nuclear disarmament will almost certainly degenerate into an unstable rearmament race. Thus, despite the desirability of a world without nuclear weapons, an agreement to that end does not appear feasible either today or for the foreseeable future.

REAGAN: SUBSTITUTE DEFENSIVE FORCES FOR OFFENSIVE FORCES

On March 23, 1983, President Reagan proposed his solution to the problem of security in the nuclear age. He launched the Strategic Defense Initiative (SDI), a vast program that promised to create an impenetrable shield to protect the entire nation against a missile attack and therefore remove the need to threaten nuclear retaliation in order to deter attack. Indeed, with the shield in place, the President argued, we would be able to discard not just nuclear deterrence but nuclear weapons themselves.

From his March 23 speech to the present, the President has continually suggested that Star Wars, as the program has come to be known, will shield populations from nuclear weapons attacks and free us from a strategy of deterrence. In his original statement Reagan said:

I've become more and more deeply convinced that the human spirit must be capable of rising above dealing with other nations and human beings by threatening their existence.

. . . Let me share with you a vision of the future which offers hope. It is that we embark on a program to counter the awesome Soviet missile threat with measures that are defensive.

. . . What if free people could live secure in the knowledge that their security did not rest upon the threat of instant U.S. retaliation to deter a Soviet attack, that we could intercept and destroy strategic ballistic missiles before they reached our own soil or that of our allies?

. . . isn't it worth every investment necessary to free the world from the threat of nuclear war?

. . . I call upon the scientific community in our country, those who gave us nuclear weapons, to turn their great talents now to the cause of mankind and world peace, to give us the means of rendering these nuclear weapons impotent and obsolete.

. . . This could pave the way for arms control measures to eliminate the weapons themselves.

More recent statements by the President show that he has not shied away from his promise of a perfect defense and a new strategy based on a nuclear-free world. On March 29, 1985, Reagan said:

We seek to render obsolete the balance of terror—or mutual assured destruction, as it's called—and replace it with a system incapable of initiating armed conflict or causing mass destruction, yet effective in preventing war.

On August 22, 1985, he said:

> Looking to the future, we're moving forward with re-
> search on a project that offers us a way out of our nuclear
> dilemma—the one that has confounded mankind for four
> decades now. The Strategic Defense Initiative research
> program offers us the hope of protecting ourselves and our
> allies from a nuclear ballistic missile attack.

Following the 1985 Geneva Summit, Reagan told a joint session of Congress about his meeting with Gorbachev:

> I described our Strategic Defense Initiative, our research
> effort, that envisions the possibility of defensive systems
> which could ultimately protect all nations against the
> danger of nuclear war. . . . If our research succeeds
> . . . nations could defend themselves against missile attack
> and mankind, at long last, escape the prison of mutual
> terror.

The President and his Secretary of Defense, Caspar Weinberger, continue to promise that this strategic revolution is at
hand.

Virtually all others associated with the SDI have recognized
and admitted that such a leakproof defense is so far in the
future, if indeed it ever proves feasible, that it offers no solution
to our present dilemma. Indeed, Lieutenant General James
Abrahamson, director of the SDI organization, has stated, "A
perfect astrodome defense is not a realistic thing." Abrahamson has also testified, "Nowhere have we stated that the goal
of the SDI is to come up with a 'leakproof' defense." Thus,
Abrahamson and virtually every other Administration official,

save for Reagan and Weinberger, advocate missions for a Star
Wars system other than a perfect "security shield." These
alternative aims range from defense of "hardened" targets
(targets reinforced with steel and concrete—for example, missile silos and command centers) to partial protection of our
population.

For the sake of clarity I will call these alternative programs
Star Wars II, to distinguish them from the President's original
proposal, which will be labeled Star Wars I. It is essential to
understand that these two versions of Star Wars have diametri-
cally opposite objectives. The President's program, if achieved,
would substitute defensive for offensive forces. In contrast,
Star Wars II systems have one characteristic in common: they
would all require that we continue to maintain offensive forces
but add the defensive systems to them.

Before discussion of Star Wars II, it would be useful to
examine why the President's original proposal, Star Wars I,
will prove an unattainable dream in our lifetime.

The reason is clear. There is no evidence that any combination of the "defensive technologies" now on the most visionary
of horizons can undo the revolution wrought by the invention
of nuclear explosives. "War" is only one of the concepts whose
meanings were changed forever at Hiroshima. "Defense" is
another. Before Hiroshima, defense relied on attrition—ex-
hausting an enemy's human, material, and moral resources.
The Royal Air Force won the Battle of Britain by attaining a
10 percent attrition rate against the Nazi Luftwaffe, because
repeated attacks could not be sustained against such odds. The
converse, a 90 percent effective defense, could not preserve us
against even one modest nuclear attack.

This example illustrates that strategic defense in the missile
age is prodigiously difficult at best, an impression that is borne
out by a detailed examination of all the schemes that propose

to mount defenses in space. The term "defensive technologies" may conjure up images of mighty fortifications, but it refers to delicate instruments: huge mirrors of exquisite precision, ultrasensitive detectors of heat and radiation, optical systems that must find and aim at a one-foot target thousands of miles away, moving at four miles per second, and so forth.* All these marvels must work near the theoretical limit of perfection; even small losses in precision would lead to unacceptably poor performance. Quite feeble blows by one's opponent against the orbiting "battle stations" bearing such crown jewels of technology could render them useless.

Such attacks need not be surgical. If the Soviets were about to demolish us with a nuclear attack, they would surely not shrink from first destroying our unmanned space platforms. And they have had nuclear-armed antiballistic missile interceptors—similar to those deployed around Moscow under the provisions of the 1972 ABM Treaty that are ideally suited to that task—for two decades. Such weapons could punch a large hole in our shield of space platforms, through which the Soviet first strike could immediately be launched. Hence, any defense based on orbiting platforms is fatally vulnerable, or, as Edward Teller, one of the most ardent proponents of antimissile systems, has put it, "Lasers in space won't fill the bill—they must be deployed in great numbers at terrible cost and could be destroyed in advance of an attack." The wide variety of countermeasures that have been developed during decades of ABM research show that every other proposed space defense scheme has its own Achilles' heel.

Moreover, to fully protect the United States from Soviet nuclear attack, defenses against ballistic missiles would be insufficient. We would have to undertake parallel development

---

*A brief technical discussion of the elements of a Star Wars defense system is included in Appendix V.

of defenses against nuclear weapons delivered by low-flying cruise missiles and by bomber aircraft. These technical tasks would be every bit as formidable as devising a defense against ballistic missile weapons. Even then, as Under Secretary of Defense Fred Iklé has acknowledged, "you cannot protect a city against a smuggled bomb done by a power in control of nuclear weapons." Thus, in the words of Major General John Toomay, a member of the President's Defensive Technologies Study Team (the Fletcher panel), "no imaginable set of defenses can prevent a determined and resourceful enemy from detonating nuclear weapons in our country."

The prospect of achieving the goal of Star Wars I has been succinctly put by Robert S. Cooper, the Pentagon's director of advanced research in the first term of the Reagan Administration: "There is no combination of gold or platinum bullets that we see in our technology arsenal . . . that would make it possible to do away with our strategic offensive ICBM forces."

The cost of either a Star Wars I or II system would be immense. As Secretary Weinberger has said, it is difficult to estimate the cost of a system that is only in the conceptual stage. But enough is known to indicate the magnitude of the project. Richard De Lauer, President Reagan's former under secretary of defense for research and engineering, has said, "When the time comes that you deploy any one of these technologies, you'll be staggered at the cost that they will involve." He added that development of each of the eight elements of a ballistic missile defense system (e.g., the kill mechanism, the sensors, the battle-management computers, and the aiming and tracking systems) is individually as complex as the Manhattan Project. A 1982 Pentagon study estimated that a space-based laser defense aimed at preventing missile attacks on the United States would cost $500 billion. Former

Secretaries of Defense James Schlesinger and Harold Brown have each estimated the cost of a full-scale effort to defend populations to be $1 trillion. I would add that whatever the cost of testing and deploying a large-scale Star Wars I or Star Wars II system, that massive expenditure would not constitute a final price tag. We would, for the rest of time, have to constantly upgrade and augment the Star Wars system in response to the demands of the arms competition and new technologies. If we move toward deployment, Star Wars will require an annual expenditure of between $100 billion and $200 billion. Thus, to deploy Star Wars would force us to divert massive amounts of money from conventional defense and from domestic programs over a period of years extending well beyond the end of this century.

Until there are inventions that have not yet even been imagined, a defense robust and cheap enough to replace deterrence will remain a pipe dream. Given that harsh reality, President Reagan's claims that defensive forces are "morally preferable" to offensive forces and that we have a "moral obligation" to pursue them are, as James Schlesinger has put it, "pernicious." Schlesinger adds that "in our lifetime and that of our children, cities will be protected by the forebearance of those on the other side, or through effective deterrence." Harold Brown, who succeeded Edward Teller as director of the Lawrence Livermore Laboratory, agrees. He said: "Technology does not offer even a reasonable prospect of a successful population defense. . . . Both the United States and the Soviet Union will be able to undertake successful countermeasures against any system intended to defend urban-industrial centers and their populations—however many the layers of defense." Thus, "mutual assured destruction" is not, as some have alleged, an immoral policy. Mutual assured destruction—the

vulnerability of each superpower to the awesome destructive
power of nuclear weapons—is not a policy at all. It is a grim
fact of life.

STRENGTHEN DETERRENCE

Former Secretary of State Henry Kissinger agrees that achieve-
ment of Star Wars I in any time period relevant to our current
problem is impossible. But Kissinger has become a supporter
of Star Wars II—deploying strategic defenses while maintaining our offensive systems. He has written: "Even granting—as
I do—that a perfect defense of our population is almost certainly unattainable, the existence of some defense means that
the attacker must plan on saturating it. This massively compli-
cates the attacker's calculations. Anything that magnifies
doubt inspires hesitation and adds to deterrence. The case
grows stronger if one considers the defense of Intercontinental
Ballistic Missile (ICBM) launchers. . . . The incentive for a first
strike would be sharply, perhaps decisively, reduced if an aggressor knew that half of the opponent's ICBMs would survive
any foreseeable attack." Other prominent supporters of Star
Wars II include former national security advisor Zbigniew
Brzezinski and Max Kampelman, now the chief U.S. arms
negotiator, who, in a jointly written essay, stated, "The combination of defense against space missiles with retaliatory offense
in reserve enhances deterrence."

But one need not turn to outside experts to find support for
Star Wars II. If not for the rhetoric of Reagan and Weinberger, one could easily conclude that Star Wars II is indeed
the essence of the administration's Strategic Defense Initiative. Lieutenant General Abrahamson, who directs SDI, has
stated, "In pursuing strategic defenses it has never been our
goal to eventually give up our policy of deterrence." According

to a booklet issued by the White House in January 1985, "Providing a better, more stable basis for enhanced deterrence is the central purpose of the SDI program." Fred Hoffman, director of the President's Future Security Strategy Study Team, whose aim was to set the policy goals for SDI, has stated, "The relevant question for the foreseeable future is not whether defenses should replace offensive weapons but whether a combination of militarily effective and discriminating offense and defenses will better meet our strategic requirements for deterrence and limiting damage." A declassified version of National Security Decision Directive 172, signed by the President on May 30, 1985, stated, "For the foreseeable future, offensive nuclear forces and the prospect of nuclear retaliation will remain the key element of deterrence." Paul Nitze, the President's special advisor on arms control matters, has said, "[we] accept the continuing need for reliance on offensive weapons and the ultimate threat of devastating retaliation as the basis for deterrence."

Not only Kampelman and Nitze, but virtually every other policymaker in the Reagan Administration agrees with Kissinger that a leakproof defense of population that would allow the elimination of nuclear weapons is not in the cards. Therefore, while the President and the Secretary of Defense adhere to their original proposal, the technicians and others working on the SDI program are producing less radical rationales that blur critical distinctions between defense of missiles and command centers, which might be technically feasible, and comprehensive defense, which is not. These ever-shifting and intermingled rationales for Star Wars II call for careful scrutiny.

The most powerful argument put forward by those who favor "offense plus defense" is that presented by Kissinger: even a partially effective defense would introduce a vital element of uncertainty into Soviet attack plans and would thereby enhance deterrence. This assumes that the Soviet military's sole concern is to attack us and that any uncertainty in their minds is therefore to our advantage. But any suspicions they may harbor about our wishing to achieve a first-strike capability —and, as I said before and will discuss more fully later, they do indeed hold such views—would be inflamed by a partially effective defense. Moreover, there are much cheaper and less dangerous ways of achieving the same objective.

Why will the Soviets suspect that Star Wars II is designed to support a first-strike strategy? Because a leaky umbrella offers no protection in a downpour but is quite useful in a drizzle. That is, such a defense would collapse under a full-scale Soviet first strike but might cope adequately with the depleted Soviet forces that had survived a U.S. first strike.

And that is what causes the problem. President Reagan, in a little-remembered sentence in his March 23, 1983, speech, said, "If paired with offensive systems, [defensive systems] can be viewed as fostering an aggressive policy, and no one wants that." The President was concerned that the Soviets would regard a decision to supplement—rather than replace—our offensive forces with defenses as an attempt to achieve a first-strike capability. Reagan has subsequently said, "I think that would be the most dangerous thing in the world, for either one of us to be seen as having the capacity for a first strike." But that is exactly how the Soviets are interpreting our program, which despite the President's concern appears aimed precisely at "pairing" offensive systems with defenses.

Americans often find it incredible that the Soviets could suspect us of such monstrous intentions, especially since we did not attack them when we enjoyed overwhelming nuclear superiority (note the data in Appendix IV).

This view, that the Soviets can trust us, pervades the statements of Reagan and Weinberger. "In 1946," Reagan has said, "when the United States was the only country in the world possessing these awesome nuclear weapons, we did not blackmail others with threats to use them. . . . Doesn't our record alone refute the charge that we seek superiority, that we represent a threat to peace?" Weinberger has stated that the Soviets "know perfectly well that we will never launch a first strike on the Soviet Union." Reagan told Soviet journalists visiting the White House, "I can assure you now we are not going to try and monopolize [the SDI], if such a weapon is developed, for a first-strike capability."

While I share the President's belief that the United States does not today, and has not ever in the past, had a first-strike strategy, we cannot fault the Soviets for thinking otherwise.

For example, a declassified 1954 document reveals that General Curtis LeMay, head of the Strategic Air Command, stated, "I believe that if the U.S. is pushed in the corner far enough we would not hesitate to strike first." And as I noted in Chapter 3, in a November 1962 memorandum to President Kennedy I stated that the Air Force proposals for the 1964 fiscal year budget were based on the objective of achieving a first-strike capability.

In the memorandum I reaffirmed my belief that a first-strike strategy should be rejected as a U.S. policy objective, and it was. But the Soviets must have heard the Air Force's position put forward in the corridors of Washington; they saw our forces building at a rate that they could have interpreted as consistent with a first-strike capability; and they did not know of my recommendation to the President or of his decision.

More recently, they have seen the United States, while facing the most serious fiscal crisis in its history, decide to procure fifty very expensive MX missiles. These are to be deployed in Minuteman silos that Secretary Weinberger says are vulnerable to Soviet attack. The Soviets can think of only one rational explanation for such a decision, i.e., the missiles are to be part of a U.S. first-strike force, in which case they will not be in the vulnerable silos if and when the Soviets retaliate.

In any event, it is the Administration's view that the Soviets can trust us. At the same time, however, a prime justification for SDI has been that we can't trust them, for they *do* seek a first-strike capability and they *would* exploit a strategic advantage.

According to President Reagan, the Soviets believe a nuclear war is "winnable, which means that they believe that if you could achieve enough superiority, then your opponent wouldn't have retaliatory strike capacity."

And Assistant Secretary of Defense Richard Perle has testified:

Lack of an effective ABM defense today is really the missing link of the Soviet warfighting potential. And it should be noted here that the Soviet doctrine and military plans call for developing a warfighting capability, in contrast to US defense doctrine which is based on development of sufficient military capability for effective deterrence of war. . . . Only through the deployment of large scale ballistic missile defense can the Soviets hope to prevent—rather than limit damage from—retaliatory attacks against important military targets and political targets.

Secretary Weinberger has said, "I can't imagine a more destabilizing factor for the world than if the Soviets should acquire a thoroughly reliable defense against these missiles before we do." Weinberger has also stated, "I cannot imagine that the Soviets, if they had a monopoly position, would do anything other than try to blackmail the rest of the world."

And on another occasion he pointed to the Soviet expenditures on antimissile programs as indicating that "the Soviets are seeking a first-strike capability."

It is clear that both sides deeply distrust each other. As I have said, not only do the Soviets know that a first strike was not always excluded from U.S. strategic thinking, but they also have reason to doubt Reagan's assertion that the United States did not and would not exploit a nuclear monopoly or nuclear superiority. They recall not only Hiroshima and Nagasaki, but subsequent threats to use nuclear weapons by, among others, Harry Truman (Korea), Dwight Eisenhower (also Korea), Richard Nixon (Vietnam), and Jimmy Carter (Persian Gulf).

Nor are the Soviets likely to accept Reagan's pledge to share SDI technology with the Soviet Union in order to ensure that the program will not lead to a U.S. unilateral advantage.

Secretary Weinberger and Lieutenant General Abrahamson, anxious to sell SDI to Congress and to U.S. allies, have stressed the benefits of SDI technology not only for missile defenses, but also for other military and civilian purposes. Will we provide the Soviets with technology that will help them to prosecute wars more effectively, whether with conventional or nuclear forces, in Afghanistan or Europe? Will we give them the most advanced computers—far superior to anything available to either the East or West today—and thus undermine our competitive position in the commercial markets of the world? It was only two years ago that we refused to license the sale to the USSR of relatively simple personal computers.

It is inconceivable that our government would share our most advanced technology with the Soviet Union in the ab-

sence of a dramatic change in the superpower political relationship. And if a change of such magnitude occurred, there would
be no need for new military hardware.

Reagan's claim that we will give SDI to the Soviets, in light
of U.S. efforts to prevent even our staunch ally Britain from
sharing fully in the fruits of the SDI research in which they
are participating, is utterly incredible.

And what are we to make of the following statement by
Lieutenant General Abrahamson: "I think it is imperative that
we have a much more effective defense than they have."

Abrahamson's remark can only increase Soviet fears that
through SDI the United States aims to regain strategic superiority. There have been other indications. Secretary Weinberger has testified:

> If we can get a system which is effective and which we
> know can render their weapons impotent, we would be
> back in a situation we were in, for example, when we were
> the only nation with the nuclear weapon and we did not
> threaten others with it.

The Soviets have made their view of SDI clear. According
to General Secretary Gorbachev: "Talk of its supposed defensive nature is, of course, a fairy tale for the gullible. The idea
is to attempt to paralyze the Soviet Union's strategic arms and
guarantee the opportunity of an unpunished nuclear strike
against our country." Following the November 1985 Geneva
summit, Gorbachev evaluated the U.S. position:

> They say: Believe us, if the Americans were the first to
> implement the SDI, they would share their experience
> with the Soviet Union. I then said: Mr. President, I call
> on you to believe us. We have said we will not be the first

to use nuclear weapons and we would not attack the United States. Why then do you, while preserving the defense capability on Earth and underwater, intend to start the arms race also in space? You don't believe us? This shows you don't. Why should we believe you more than you believe us?

If the Soviets do not accept the statements of those who support Star Wars II—SDI is not part of a first-strike strategy but only a means of strengthening deterrence—how will they respond?

It would be foolhardy to dismiss as mere propaganda the Soviet's repeated warnings that a nationwide U.S. strategic defense is highly provocative. Their promise to respond with a large offensive buildup is no empty threat. Each superpower's highest priority has been a nuclear arsenal that can assuredly penetrate to its opponent's vital assets. Such a capability, each side believes, is needed to deter the other side from launching a nuclear attack or using a nuclear advantage for political gain.

We have said we would respond to a Soviet strategic defense plan in exactly the same way they have stated they would respond to ours. Secretary Weinberger, in November 1985, in a letter to the President, wrote, "Even a probable [Soviet] territorial defense would require us to increase the number of our offensive forces and their ability to penetrate Soviet defenses to assure that our operational plans could be executed."

Weinberger has also flatly acknowledged that the Soviets would undertake a similar response to deployment of U.S. Star Wars weapons. He told a Senate committee in 1985, "I think they will try to overwhelm or otherwise defeat a strategic defense. We are aware of that."

We can safely conclude, therefore, from both the U.S. and Soviet statements, that any attempt to strengthen deterrence by adding strategic defenses to strategic offensive forces will lead to a rapid escalation of the arms race.

The Soviet response to our SDI deployment will be based on traditional worst-case analysis, which will inevitably overestimate the effectiveness of our defense, just as in the 1960s and 1970s we targeted many more warheads on Moscow as soon as it was surrounded by ABM defenses of dubious reliability.

We would feel compelled to respond to their offensive buildup with one of our own.

And if Star Wars leads to weapons in space, the competition would extend beyond the buildup of new missiles and antimissiles. Space weapons would be vulnerable to direct attack by an array of antisatellite weapons, the technologies for which we can already envision. Harold Brown has noted that Star Wars systems would be less effective in attacking missiles than they would be in attacking the opponent's Star Wars weapons.

Thus, each side would develop not only missiles and antimissiles, but also anti-antimissiles, anti-anti-antimissiles, and so on. We could never say that the deployment of the system had been completed. It would require endless upgrades, offensive countermeasures, and satellite-survivability programs. In short, an endless arms race.

The danger that a Star Wars II defense would accelerate the arms race was recognized by the President's Defensive Technologies Study Team. It warned early on that the effectiveness and risks of a Star Wars system "will depend not only on the technology itself, but also on the extent to which the Soviet Union either agrees to mutual defense arrangements or offense limitations."

To meet the threat of arms escalation, Paul Nitze has articulated a new U.S. "strategic concept" for a cooperative shift to a Star Wars world: "What we have in mind is a jointly managed transition, one in which the United States and the

Soviet Union would together phase in new defenses in a controlled manner while continuing to reduce offensive nuclear arms." But as James Schlesinger has written, Nitze's plan "is less a strategic concept than a rationalization for the President's vision. The concept in itself is fundamentally flawed."

Although Nitze has made clear that strategic defensive forces should not be deployed other than in accordance with the terms of an arms control agreement, no human mind has conceived of how to write such a treaty. Nitze himself has said that the transition to Star Wars would be "tricky."

Why is that so?

Arms control has been difficult enough when it has had to deal only with large offensive forces whose capabilities are relatively clear. It would be vastly harder to strike a bargain over space defenses whose effectiveness would be a deep mystery even to their owners, since those systems could not be tested under remotely realistic conditions.

The congressional Office of Technology Assessment released a comprehensive study of missile defense weaponry in 1985. The report had this to say about an arms control regime that would allow for increased defenses and reduced offenses:

The negotiability of any such agreement is very much in question. Nobody has suggested how the problems of measuring, comparing, and monitoring disparate stragetic forces—problems which have plagued past arms control negotiations—could be satisfactorily resolved in the far more difficult situation where both offensive and defensive forces must be included. . . .

An arms control agreement for phasing in BMD [ballistic missile defense] would have to establish acceptable levels and types of offensive and defensive capabilities for each side and means for verifying them adequately. It would have to specify offensive system limitations that prevented either side from obtaining a superior capability to penetrate the other's defenses. It would have to specify the BMD system designs for each side that would not exceed the BMD capabilities agreed to. It is important to note, however, that no one has as yet specified in any detail just how such an arms control agreement could be formulated.

Why has no one been able to outline the content of such a treaty? Because neither U.S. nor Soviet experts can figure out how both to reduce offensive forces and permit defensive deployment, while at the same time giving each side adequate confidence in maintaining its highest goal: assuring an effective nuclear deterrent against nuclear attack.

For the sake of argument, let us consider what such an agreement might look like.

In the first paragraph the superpowers would agree to a substantial reduction in their strategic nuclear forces. The cuts might approximate 50 percent, which would leave six thousand nuclear warheads on each side. And it could be agreed that the reductions would be shaped in a way that would reduce temptations for either side to launch a first strike in a crisis.

In the second paragraph the parties would agree that each may have a strategic defense system with a missile-intercepting capability no greater than X. The value of X must be low enough so that the deterrent effectiveness of each side's six thousand warheads would not be undermined. That is, each side would have to be confident that if its opponent launched a first strike it could survive with sufficient power to penetrate the opponent's defense and retaliate. No one has suggested how to determine X.

But if we could agree on X, the third paragraph would have

to deal with design criteria. Since we cannot rely on trust to ensure Soviet compliance with arms agreements, the agreement would have to be written so as to require that their Star Wars system be designed according to specifications that we know will not provide a missile-intercepting capability greater than X. Because we could never be certain of the capabilities of our own system, this, too, is impossible.

And then even if the two sides could agree on design specifications, the treaty would have to provide for extremely intrusive inspection procedures—far more than either side would need to verify limits on offensive systems—to ensure that the defense system adhered to the specified design.

In my view, such an agreement would be impossible to reach, whatever SDI research ultimately reveals is technologically feasible. And even if in some euphoric state of good relations the superpowers did sign such an accord to reduce offenses and permit defenses, it would quickly collapse under the weight of worst-case planning and mutual fears of inferiority.

Key members of the Reagan Administration must surely realize that a controlled transition to Star Wars is not conceivable under foreseeable circumstances. Paul Nitze has acknowledged that "the Soviets have given absolutely no encouragement to such a concept."

So what is the Administration's backup plan?

Unmistakably, it is to go it alone. If the Soviets will not accept our plan—a plan that we do not yet have and almost certainly cannot produce—for a cooperative shift to Star Wars, we will settle for an uncontrolled competition. President Reagan, who once stated that the United States would not deploy Star Wars without agreement to eliminate offensive weapons, quickly recanted, telling journalists, "Obviously, if . . . we had a defensive system and we could not get agreement on their part to eliminate the nuclear weapons, we would have done our best and, no, we would go ahead with deployment." Secretary Weinberger's fiscal year 1987 report to the Congress states, "Of course, we would not under any circumstances give the Soviets a veto over our future defensive deployments." And according to SDI director Abrahamson, "While this transition period could be made easier by Soviet cooperation, it does not require cooperation."

A unilateral shift to Star Wars would have disastrous consequences. The ABM Treaty, the most important arms control agreement of the nuclear age, would be the first casualty. Because of the resulting race in strategic defense weaponry, each side would begin to build up its offenses to ensure deterrent capability. Thus, the existing SALT agreements would be the next casualty. Future accords to restrain the offensive arms competition would be impossible until the Star Wars race was halted and reversed.

It can be said without qualification: we cannot have both Star Wars and arms control.

Moreover, unilateral U.S. deployment of Star Wars weaponry, while it would incur serious risks, is unlikely to provide any tangible benefits to U.S. security. The Soviets will almost certainly match our strategic defenses with their own defenses of at least comparable capability. Under almost any scenario, such Soviet defenses would cancel out the security advantages we hoped to gain through our deployments.

In sum, I can see no way by which U.S. deployment of an antiballistic missile defense will strengthen deterrence.

But assume for a moment that were not the case. Is there an alternative means of achieving Henry Kissinger's goal? He fears the Soviets have now, or will achieve in the future, a first-strike capability. It is that which he is trying to offset or prevent. Can that be accomplished at less cost, with greater certainty, and with less risk of fueling the arms race by some means other than the SDI?

President Reagan's Commission on Strategic Forces, headed by Lieutenant General Scowcroft, stated that we do not face a Soviet first-strike threat today, since the vulnerability of our strategic forces—land- and submarine-based missiles and bomber weapons—"should be assessed collectively and not in isolation." Moreover, they believed we could avoid such a threat in the future. Their proposal for doing so is far less costly, far less risky, and far more likely to enhance our security than deployment of any form of ballistic missile defense. It is based on the simple approach of reducing the ratio of the number of accurate Soviet warheads to the number of our vulnerable land-based missiles. This could be done through negotiation with the Soviet Union or by replacing our potentially vulnerable fixed-base missiles (Minutemen) with mobile missiles (Midgetmen), or by a combination of the two approaches. Gorbachev has already indicated a willingness to move in this direction if we would by similar moves reduce our threat to his forces.

Having rebutted the argument that Star Wars is needed to enhance deterrence, I should deal, perhaps, with other arguments that are sometimes put forward in support of the Strategic Defense Initiative.

It has been said that a limited strategic defense is needed to intercept small nuclear-missile attacks by Third World countries or terrorist groups or from a Soviet accidental launch. But small countries or liberation groups, if they did manage to acquire a nuclear weapon, are far more likely to deliver it by the smuggled suitcase bomb than by the long-range ballistic missile. The best way to prevent nuclear threats from the Third World is not to build a missile defense that will reignite the superpower arms race but to continue to work with the Soviets and other nations to halt the spread of nuclear weapons to additional countries.

Nor is a provocative Star Wars system the best solution to the accidental-launch problem. We have paid and should continue to pay attention to preventing accidents on our side and encourage the Soviets to do the same. Moreover, the superpowers could place remote-control devices on their missiles that would disarm them and prevent them from exploding in the event of accidental launch.

A further rationale for an imperfect defense is that it will limit damage to our society if nuclear war occurs. But the Soviet arsenal is already so vast that even a 95 percent effective defense, which no administration official is promising, would allow some five hundred nuclear ballistic missile warheads— not to mention bomber and cruise missile weapons—to explode on the United States. Gerard Smith, President Nixon's arms control negotiator, has said: "No responsible official could suggest that, with such a system in place, nuclear war was any more acceptable than it is today. The only way to protect our country from nuclear war is to prevent nuclear war."

And, finally, one could argue that the United States could use Star Wars II to do precisely what the Soviets accuse us of doing—gain a technical lead over the Soviets, thereby achieving nuclear superiority for the United States. Indeed, George Keyworth, Reagan's former science advisor, once wrote that with SDI we will "play our trump—technological leverage." Those who hold this view ignore post-Hiroshima history and have less respect than I for the Soviet regime's ability to match our weapons and extract sacrifices from its people.

The U.S. invention of the atomic bomb was the most remarkable technical breakthrough in military history. And yet the Soviet Union, though devastated by war and operating from a technological base far weaker than ours, was able to create nuclear forces that gave it a plausible deterrent in an astonishingly short time. As I argued in Chapter 3, virtually every technical initiative in the nuclear arms race has come from the United States, but the net result has been a steady erosion of American security. There is no evidence that space weapons will be an exception.

If all this is true, why are the Soviets so worried by Star Wars? Because they fear that strategic defense could give us an edge if they played dead. For that reason they must respond. This will require vast expenditures they can ill afford, and will ultimately diminish their security. But that is equally true for us, whether we recognize it or not.

To summarize, none of these rationales for Star Wars II offer a satisfactory approach to reducing the risk of nuclear war in the decades that lie ahead. They combine unattainable technical goals with a policy rooted in concepts whose validity died at Hiroshima. And they carry the certainty of high cost and a dangerous escalation of the arms race.

We are left, then, to turn to our final option: a reexamination of the military role of nuclear weapons.

BASE WAR PLANS AND ARMS CONTROL AGREEMENTS ON THE BELIEF THAT NUCLEAR WARHEADS ARE NOT USABLE WEAPONS

In Chapter 1, when discussing NATO's current strategy, which is based on deterrence of Soviet conventional aggression by the threat of initiating the use of nuclear weapons, I stated that no one had ever developed a plan for initiating the use of such weapons with benefit to NATO. More and more military and civilian leaders are publicly acknowledging this fact.

Field Marshal Lord Carver, Chief of the British Defence Staff from 1973 to 1976, repudiates the officially approved NATO strategy. He is totally opposed to NATO ever initiating the use of nuclear weapons. Lord Carver wrote in the London *Sunday Times* of February 21, 1982:

> At the theater or tactical level any nuclear exchange, however limited it might be, is bound to leave NATO worse off in comparison to the Warsaw Pact, in terms both of military and civilian casualties and destruction. . . . the only exception would be if the Soviet Union were to respond to NATO's use of nuclear weapons either with a much more limited response or none at all. To initiate use of nuclear weapons on that assumption seems to me to be criminally irresponsible.

Admiral Noel A. Gayler, former Commander in Chief of U.S. ground, air, and sea forces in the Pacific, agrees with Lord Carver: "There is no sensible military use of any of our nuclear forces. Their only reasonable use is to deter our opponent from using his nuclear forces."

General Johannes Steinhoff, the former Luftwaffe Chief of Staff, offers much the same view as Admiral Gayler: "I am in favor of retaining nuclear weapons as potential tools, but not permitting them to become battlefield weapons. I am not opposed to the strategic employment of these weapons; however, I am firmly opposed to their tactical use on our soil."

As I mentioned in Chapter 2, former Secretary of State Henry Kissinger, speaking in Brussels in 1979, made quite clear he did not believe the U.S. would ever initiate a nuclear strike against the Soviet Union: "Our European allies should not keep asking us to multiply strategic assurances that we cannot possibly mean or if we do mean, we should not want to execute because if we execute, we risk the destruction of civilization."

Melvin Laird, Secretary of Defense in the Nixon Administration, declared himself unequivocally in favor of a nonnuclear world and very clearly aligned himself with Lord Carver, Admiral Gayler, and General Steinhoff. He said, "These weapons— are useless for military purposes."

By implication, President Reagan, in March 1983, when proposing a program to develop an antiballistic missile defense, questioned the necessity of maintaining the threat of first use of nuclear weapons. As you will recall, his theme was that our objective should be to move to an impenetrable defense against Soviet nuclear strikes, thereby totally neutralizing their offensive nuclear forces. And he added that it would be in our interest for the Soviets to possess a similar defense.

The President was stating, in effect, that the Soviet Union and the United States would both be better off if nuclear weapons were totally eliminated. Under such circumstances NATO would depend, of course, solely on conventional forces for deterrence of Soviet aggression.

The President made an even more categorical statement in favor of a nonnuclear world when he said on June 16, 1983, "I pray for the day when nuclear weapons will no longer exist anywhere on earth." And he reaffirmed this position in his address to the nation on February 26, 1986, when he stated, "Our goal should be to deter, and if necessary to repel, any aggression without a resort to nuclear arms."

If there is a case for NATO retaining its present strategy, that case must rest on the strategy's contribution to the deterrence of Soviet aggression being worth the risk of nuclear war in the event deterrence fails.

The question of what deters Soviet aggression is an extremely difficult one. To answer it we must put ourselves in the minds of the several individuals who would make the decision to initiate war. We must ask what their objectives are for themselves and their nation, what they value and they fear. We must assess their proclivity to take risks, to bluff, or to be bluffed. We must guess how they see us—our will and our capabilities—and determine what we can do to strengthen their belief in the sincerity of our threats and our promises.

But most difficult of all, we must evaluate all these factors in the context of an acute international crisis. Our problem is not to persuade the Soviets not to initiate war today. It is to cause them to reach the same decision at some future time when, for whatever reason—for example, an uprising in Eastern Europe that is getting out of control, or a U.S.-Soviet clash in Iran, or conflict in the Middle East—they may be tempted to gamble and try to end what they see as a great threat to their own security.

In such a crisis, perceptions of risks and stakes may change substantially. What may look like a reckless gamble in more tranquil times might be seen then merely as a reasonable risk. This will be the case particularly if the crisis deteriorates so that war begins to appear more and more likely. In such a situation, the advantages of achieving tactical surprise by going first can appear to be more and more important.

As I have indicated, the launch of strategic nuclear weapons against the Soviet homeland would lead almost certainly to a response in kind that would inflict unacceptable damage on Europe and the United States—it would be an act of suicide. The threat of such an action, therefore, has lost all credibility as a deterrent to Soviet conventional aggression. The ultimate sanction in the flexible-response strategy is thus no longer operative. One cannot build a credible deterrent on an incredible action.

Many sophisticated observers in both the United States and Europe, however, believe that the threat to use tactical nuclear weapons in response to Warsaw Pact aggression increases the perceived likelihood of such an action, despite its absolute irrationality. They believe that by maintaining battlefield weapons near the front lines, along with the requisite plans and doctrines to implement the strategy that calls for their use, NATO confronts the Warsaw Pact with a dangerous possibility that cannot be ignored.

In contemplating the prospect of war, they argue, Soviet leaders must perceive a risk that NATO would implement its doctrine and use nuclear weapons on the battlefield, thus initiating an escalatory process which could easily get out of control, leading ultimately to a devastating strategic exchange between the two homelands. It is not that NATO would coolly and deliberately calculate that a strategic exchange made sense, they explain, but rather that the dynamics of the crisis would literally force such an action—or so Soviet leaders would have to fear.

Each step of the escalation would create a new reality, altering each side's calculation of the risks and benefits of alternative courses of action. Once U.S. and Soviet military units clashed, perceptions of the likelihood of more intense conflicts would be changed radically. Once any nuclear weapon had been used operationally, assessments of other potential nuclear attacks would be radically altered.

In short, those who assert that the nuclear first-use threat serves to strengthen NATO's deterrent believe that, regardless of objective assessments of the irrationality of any such action, Soviet decision-makers must pay attention to the realities of the battlefield and the dangers of the escalatory process. And, in so doing, they maintain, the Soviets will perceive a considerable risk that conventional conflict will lead to the use of battlefield weapons, which will lead in turn to theater-wide nuclear conflict, which will inevitably spread to the homelands of the superpowers.

In fact, as I pointed out in Chapter 3, it was the desire to strengthen the perception of such a likely escalation that led NATO to its December 1979 decision to deploy the new intermediate-range Pershing II and the nuclear-armed cruise missiles in Europe. The key element in that decision was that the new missiles would be capable of striking Soviet territory, thus presumably precipitating a Soviet attack on U.S. territory and a U.S. retaliation against the whole of the Soviet home-land. The new weapons thus "couple" U.S. strategic forces with the forces deployed in Europe, easing concerns that the Soviets might perceive a firebreak in the escalatory process. So long as the escalation is perceived to be likely to proceed smoothly, the logic continues, then the Warsaw Pact will be deterred from taking the first step—the conventional aggres-sion—which might start the process.

But the flaw in the reasoning, as I argued earlier, is that a U.S. President would be just as reluctant to launch missiles from European soil against Soviet territory as he would be to initiate the use of U.S.-based strategic nuclear weapons against the USSR.

And, as I have indicated, more and more Western political and military leaders are coming to recognize, and publicly avowing, that even the use of battlefield nuclear weapons in Europe would bring greater destruction to NATO than any conceivable contribution they might make to NATO's de-fense.

There is less and less likelihood, therefore, that NATO would authorize the use of any nuclear weapons—whether they be tactical or strategic—except in response to a Soviet nuclear attack. As this diminishing prospect becomes more and more widely perceived—and it will—whatever deterrent value still resides in NATO's nuclear strategy will diminish still further.

There are additional factors to be considered. Whether it contributes to deterrence or not, NATO's threat of first use is not without its costs. It is a most contentious policy, leading to divisive debates both within individual nations and between the members of the Alliance; it reduces NATO's preparedness for conventional war; and, as I have indicated, it increases the risk of nuclear war.

Preparing for tactical nuclear war limits NATO's ability to defend itself conventionally in several ways. Nuclear weapons are indeed "special" munitions. They require special security precautions. They limit the flexibility with which units can be deployed and military plans altered. Operations on a nuclear battlefield would be very different than those in a conventional conflict. NATO planning must take these differences into account.

Moreover, since most of the systems that would deliver NATO's nuclear munitions are dual-purpose, some number of aircraft and artillery must be reserved to be available for nuclear attacks early in a battle, if that becomes necessary, and are thus not available for delivering conventional munitions.

Most importantly, though, the reliance on NATO's nuclear threats for deterrence makes it more difficult to muster the political and financial support necessary to sustain an adequate conventional military force. Both publics and governments point to the nuclear force as the "real deterrent," thus explaining their reluctance to allocate even modest sums for greater conventional capabilities.

To the extent that the nuclear threat has deterrent value, it is because it increases the risk that nuclear weapons will be used in the event of war. The location of nuclear weapons in what would be forward parts of the battlefield; the associated development of operational plans assuming the early use of nuclear weapons; the possibility that release authority would be delegated to field commanders prior to the outset of war—these factors and many others would lead to a higher probability that if war actually began in Europe, it would soon turn into a nuclear conflagration.

Soviet predictions of such a risk, in fact, could lead them to initiate nuclear war themselves. If the Soviets believe that NATO would indeed carry out its nuclear threat once it decided to go to war—whether as a matter of deliberate choice or because the realities of the battlefield would give the Alliance no choice—the Soviets would have virtually no incentive not to initiate nuclear war themselves.

I repeat, this would only be the case if they had decided that war was imminent and believed there would be a high risk that NATO's threats would be fulfilled. But if those two conditions were valid, the military advantages to the Warsaw Pact of preemptive nuclear strikes on NATO's nuclear storage sites, delivery systems, and support facilities could be compelling.

The costs of whatever deterrent value remains in NATO's nuclear strategy are, therefore, substantial. Could not equivalent deterrence be achieved at lesser "cost"? I believe the answer is yes. Compared to the huge risks the Alliance now runs by relying on increasingly less credible nuclear threats, recent studies have pointed to ways by which the conventional forces may be strengthened at modest military, political, and economic cost.

A HIGH-CONFIDENCE CONVENTIONAL DEFENSE THAT IS POLITICALLY AND FINANCIALLY FEASIBLE?

Writing in *Foreign Affairs* in 1982, General Bernard Rogers, Supreme Allied Commander in Europe, stated that major improvements in NATO's conventional forces were feasible at a modest price. These improvements, he said, would permit a shift from the present strategy requiring the early use of nuclear weapons to a strategy of "no early use of nuclear weapons." General Rogers estimated the cost to be approximately 1 percent per year greater than the 3 percent annual increase (in real terms) which the members of NATO, meeting in Washington, had agreed to in 1978.

An experienced Pentagon consultant, MIT Professor William W. Kaufmann, has taken General Rogers's suggestions of 4 percent annual increases in NATO defense budgets and analyzed how those funds could best be allocated to improve the Alliance's conventional defenses. After an exhaustive analysis he concluded that a conventional force could be acquired that would be sufficiently strong to give a high probability of deterring Soviet aggression without threatening the use of nuclear weapons.

Recently, an international study group also analyzed the possibilities for moving away from NATO's present nuclear reliance. The steering committee of this European Security Study included among its members General Andrew Goodpaster, who once served as the Supreme Allied Commander in Europe; General Franz-Josef Schulze, a German officer, formerly the Commander in Chief of Allied Forces in Europe; and Air Chief Marshal Sir Alasdair Steedman, formerly the United Kingdom's military representative to NATO.

Their report concludes that NATO's conventional forces could be strengthened substantially at a very modest cost—a total of approximately $20 billion that would be spent over a period of five or six years. For comparative purposes, note that the U.S. D5 submarine-launched missile program is expected to cost $17 billion over the next five years.

The European Security Study stated that to constitute an effective deterrent NATO's conventional forces do not have to match specific Soviet capabilities. Rather, these forces need only be strong enough to create serious concerns for Warsaw Pact planners whether or not their attack could succeed.

To accomplish this, the Study concluded, NATO's conventional forces would have to be able to:

- Stop the initial Warsaw Pact attack.
- Erode the enemy's air power.
- Interdict the follow-on and reinforcing armored formations that the Pact would attempt to bring up to the front lines.
- Disrupt the Pact's command, control, and communications.

The report outlines in detail how NATO could achieve these four objectives utilizing newly available technologies and accomplishing with conventional weapons what previously had required nuclear munitions. These technological advances would permit the very accurate delivery of large numbers of conventional weapons, along with dramatic improvements in the ability to handle massive quantities of military information.

The effectiveness of the new technologies was testified to most recently by Senator Sam Nunn:

We now have at hand new conventional technologies capable of destroying the momentum of a Soviet invasion by means of isolating the first echelon of attacking forces from reinforcing follow-on echelons. These technologies . . . capitalize on three major advances. The first is the substantially improved lethality of improved conventional munitions. . . . The second is the growing capability of microelectronics to enhance the rapid collection, processing, distribution, and ability to act upon information about the size, character, location, and movement of enemy units. . . . The third is improved ability to move and target quickly large quantities of improved conventional firepower against enemy force concentrations.

The potential of any one of the several proposals for increasing the strength of the conventional forces, within reasonable financial constraints, is great. Unfortunately, not one of them has yet been accepted by any NATO nation for incorporation in its force structure and defense budget. NATO has not done so because there is today no consensus among its military and civilian leaders on the military role of nuclear weapons.

There is, however, a slow but discernible movement toward acceptance of three facts:

- NATO's existing plans for initiating the use of nuclear weapons, if implemented, are far more likely to destroy Europe than to defend it.
- Whatever deterrent value remains in NATO's nuclear strategy is eroding rapidly and is purchased at heavy cost.
- The strength, and hence the deterrent capability, of

NATO's conventional forces can be increased substantially within realistic political and financial constraints.

It is on the basis of these facts that I propose we accept that nuclear warheads are not weapons—they have no military use whatsoever except to deter one's opponent from their use—and that we base all our military plans, our defense budgets, our weapons development and deployment programs, and our arms negotiations on that proposition.

The ultimate goal should be a state of mutual deterrence at the lowest force levels consistent with stability. That requires invulnerable forces that could unquestionably respond to any attack and inflict unacceptable damage. If those forces are to remain limited, it is equally essential that they not threaten the opponent's deterrent. These factors would combine to produce a stable equilibrium in which the risk of nuclear war would be very remote.

This kind of deterrence posture should not be confused with the one currently pursued by the United States and the Soviet Union. As I have indicated, the twenty-five thousand warheads that each nation possesses did not come about through any plan. Instead, they emerged through the indiscriminate application of continuing technical innovations and the persistent failure to recognize that nuclear explosives are not weapons in any traditional sense.

If the Soviet Union and the United States were to agree, in principle, that each side's nuclear force would be no larger than was needed to deter a nuclear attack by the other, how might the size and composition of such a limited force be determined?

When discussing Gorbachev's proposal for the total elimination of nuclear weapons, I pointed out that a nuclear-free world, while desirable in principle, was infeasible under foreseeable circumstances because the fear of cheating in such an agreement would be very great indeed. I stressed, however, that policing an arms agreement that restricted each side to a small number of warheads is quite feasible with present verification technology. The number required for a force sufficiently large to deter cheating would be determined by the number the Soviets could build without detection by NATO. I know of no studies that point to what that number might be, but surely it would not exceed a few hundred, say five hundred at most. Very possibly it would be far less.

Two considerations would determine the ultimate size and composition of the deterrent force: that it deter attack with confidence, and that any undetected or sudden violation of arms control treaties would not imperil this deterrence. With tactical nuclear forces to be eliminated entirely and the strategic forces having five hundred or fewer warheads, the present inventory of fifty thousand weapons could be cut to no more than one thousand.

A reduction in U.S. and Soviet nuclear forces to levels of a few hundred warheads each may appear to be the vision of an idle dreamer. And yet while doing research for this book, I learned what I had not known before: in 1958 and 1959 the U.S. Navy put forward just such a plan. The Navy proposed an invulnerable retaliatory force of approximately 464 warheads. In the Navy's words, it would be sized by "an objective of generous adequacy for deterrence alone, not by the false goal of adequacy for 'winning.' "

Before such limited-force goals could be reached, other nuclear powers (China, France, Great Britain, and possibly others) will have to be involved in the process of reducing nuclear arsenals lest their weapons disturb the strategic equilibrium.

The proposed changes in U.S. and Soviet strategic and tactical forces would require, as would the President's SDI, complementary changes in NATO and Warsaw Pact conventional forces, or appropriate increases in NATO's conventional power. If the latter was necessary, it could be achieved at a fraction of the costs we will incur if we continue on our present course.

Having identified our goal, how can be move toward it? Some of our new policies would depend solely on the United States and its allies; others would require Soviet cooperation. The former should be governed by the dictum, attributed to President Eisenhower, that "we need what we need." Were we to drop futile war-fighting notions, we would see that many things we already have or are busily acquiring are either superfluous or downright dangerous to us, no matter what the Soviets do. Tactical nuclear weapons in Europe are a prime example, and the Administration's policy of reducing their numbers should be accelerated.

Other programs will haunt us when the Soviets copy them: sophisticated antisatellite weapons, sea-based cruise missiles, and highly accurate submarine-launched ballistic missiles. We are more dependent on satellites than the Soviets are, and more vulnerable to attack from the sea. Many of these weapons are valid bargaining chips because they threaten the Soviets, just as so much of their arsenal gratuitously threatens us. We should move quickly to refocus the arms control negotiations to accomplish what we cannot do by unilateral action alone. We can begin that process through the arms negotiations now underway in Geneva.

5.

GENEVA

A Step Toward
Our Long-Term Goal

The Geneva negotiations provide an invaluable opportunity to take a giant step toward our goals. Is that not a preposterous assertion, the reader may well ask, for have I not claimed that Star Wars, which the President refuses to abandon, precludes arms control and guarantees an arms race? Surprisingly enough, it is not, if one takes account of a remarkable speech that Paul Nitze, the Administration's senior advisor on arms control, gave in Philadelphia on February 20, 1985. If the points that Nitze made were to be accepted, it would be possible for the President to negotiate toward the goals I have set without abandoning a strategic-defense research program.

Mr. Nitze presented two criteria that must be met before the deployment of strategic defenses could be justified: the defense must work even in the face of direct attack on itself, and it must be cheaper to augment the defense than the offense.

As we have seen, nothing that satisfies these criteria is on the horizon—a judgment in which Nitze apparently concurs, for he foresaw that during an initial period of "at least the next ten years" no defenses would be deployed. During that period we would, in Nitze's words, "reverse the erosion" of the ABM Treaty.

Nitze envisioned the possibility of two additional periods following the first. In the second phase some form of Star Wars II would be deployed alongside our offensive weapons, provided the two criteria he laid down had been met. If we entered the second phase, it probably would last for at least several decades.

Ultimately, if Star Wars I proved practical, the second phase would be followed by a third, in which the leakproof shield would be deployed and offensive weapons eliminated.

As I pointed out in the previous chapter, Mr. Nitze acknowledged that the problem of how to write an arms control agreement that during the second phase would limit offensive arms while permitting defensive systems had not been solved. You will recall he said it would be "tricky." I agree. But by implication Nitze was saying that this problem—and the entire subject of deployment of defensive systems—is an issue for future negotiations and that it need not stand in the way of a new arms control agreement at this time.

That brings us back to the first phase, the window of opportunity. Why the fixation during this phase on the ABM Treaty? Because the treaty formalizes the insight that not just the deployment but even the development of strategic defenses could stimulate a buildup in offensive forces. Were the treaty to collapse, we could not move toward our goal of reducing the offensive threat. Hence the fleeting window of opportunity: strengthening of the ABM Treaty coupled with negotiations on offensive strategic forces.

The treaty forbids certain types of radars and severely restricts the testing of components of ABM systems. Both of these provisions are endangered.

The Soviets are building a radar in Siberia that appears to violate the ABM Treaty. While this radar is of marginal military significance, it has great political import and poses an issue that must be resolved to the satisfaction of the U.S. government.

In the near future the United States will be violating the

restrictions on tests in spirit—and probably in law—if we keep our research program on the schedule implied by Lieutenant General Abrahamson, the director of the SDI, when he said on March 15, 1985, that a "reasonably confident decision" on whether to build Star Wars be made by the end of the decade or in the early 1990s. If we are unwilling to refrain from the tests associated with such a schedule, the Soviets will, with good reason, assume that we are preparing to deploy defenses. They will assiduously develop their response, and the prospect for offensive arms agreements at Geneva will evaporate. The treaty's central purpose is to give each nation confidence that the other is not readying a sudden deployment of defense; we must demonstrate that we will adhere to the treaty in those terms.

We must understand that today the Soviets are guided by our actions, not our words. They hear us say the SDI is only a research program. But they see us acting in ways that they believe are consistent only with a decision, in principle, having been made already that we will unilaterally abrogate the ABM Treaty at a time of our own choosing and in a way that will place them at a strategic disadvantage.* So long as they hold that belief, there will never again be a strategic offensive-arms limitation agreement. We can change their interpretation of our actions by ensuring that the appropriations for the SDI research program, now being considered by the Congress, do not in fact permit actions contrary to the spirit of a strengthened ABM Treaty.

The existing ABM Treaty does not forbid antisatellite weapons. That loophole must also be closed. A verifiable ban on the testing of antisatellite weapons should become a part of the

---

*Even some of our words are beginning to point in the same direction. In 1984, General Abrahamson said very clearly: "It's going to go up, one piece at a time."

ABM Treaty regime. Because we are much more dependent on satellites than the Soviets are, such a ban would be very much in our interest.

A strengthened ABM Treaty would allow the Geneva negotiations to address the primary objective of offensive-arms control: increasing the stability of deterrence by eliminating the perceptions of both sides that the other has, or is seeking, a first-strike capability. This problem can be dealt with through hardheaded bargaining. There is no need to rely on the adversary's intentions: his capabilities are visible. Mutual and verifiable reductions in the ratio of each side's accurate warheads to the number of the other side's vulnerable missile launchers could reduce the first-strike threat to the point at which it would be patently incredible to everyone. Both sides have such immense forces that they should concentrate on quickly reducing the most threatening components—those that stand in the way of stability and much lower force levels.

What is needed are deep cuts in the number of warheads, but cuts shaped to eliminate the fear of first strikes. Because the two sides have such dissimilar strategic forces, the process will be very difficult, but it should be possible in the first phase to accomplish reductions of 50 percent. It would be reasonable, for example, for the United States to insist on large reductions in the number of Soviet land-based missile warheads, where they outnumber us, but in the bargaining we must be ready to make substantial cuts in our MIRVed submarine-based forces, our area of advantage.

Such an ambitious arms control agreement may seem highly unlikely in today's environment. Many U.S. officials consider it impossible. They assert, for example, that the Soviet Union is not serious about arms control. But when they do so, they overlook strong indications to the contrary.

The Soviet government was clearly interested in arms limitation throughout the 1970s, as evinced by their signing the SALT agreements, which capped the offensive arsenals, and the ABM Treaty, which put severe limits on an entire class of weaponry.

And Mikhail Gorbachev, in the brief period he has served as General Secretary, has offered numerous indications that he is prepared to put serious qualitative and quantitative limits on the arms race. He has:

- Called for a comprehensive test ban agreement, and imposed a unilateral prohibition on tests for an entire year, even though the United States did not curb its own testing program in any way.
- Put forward a proposal on intermediate-range nuclear missiles in Europe.
- Reaffirmed the view that ABM weapons must be sharply restricted, a view shared by the Johnson, Nixon, Ford, and Carter administrations.
- Joined with President Reagan in calling for a 50 percent reduction in nuclear arsenals at the November 1985 Geneva summit.

A major aim of these initiatives is no doubt to favorably impress Western public opinion. But there is strong reason to believe that the Soviets want progress in arms control. They are under great pressure to reduce the portion of their scarce resources devoted to a futile arms competition, although it is clear they will spend whatever is necessary to remain in that race.

Labeling Soviet proposals as propaganda does not serve our security interests. If Gorbachev is bluffing, let us call his bluff.

If he is sincere, we could, given sufficient political will on our side, get his signature on agreements that would benefit both the superpowers and their allies.

If we are to achieve major progress in arms control, we will have to reassess our own view of the superpower competition and the utility of nuclear weapons.

From the dawn of the nuclear age to the present, the United States has sought to maintain "superior" strategic and tactical nuclear forces—or at least forces that could give us an advantage if we, rather than the Soviets, struck the first blow. So long as we maintain this goal, it will be difficult to achieve arms control agreements aimed at a stable, low level of weapons on each side. President Reagan has already recognized and accepted this point. If we base our negotiating proposals on it, the logic of radical reductions in strategic nuclear arsenals is clear.

6.

TURNING AWAY FROM NUCLEAR DISASTER

The second half century of the nuclear age need not be a repetition of the first.

We can—we must—move away from the ad hoc decision-making of the past several decades. It is that process which has led to a world in which the two great power blocs, not yet able to avoid continuing political conflict and potential military confrontation, face each other with nuclear war-fighting strategies and nuclear arsenals capable of destroying their civilizations, and much of the rest of the world as well, several times over.

Through public debate, a debate in which citizens throughout the NATO countries—the potential victims of nuclear war —have both the capability and the responsibility of participating, we can reduce the risk of catastrophe by establishing long-term objectives that will underlie and shape all aspects of our nuclear programs: military strategy, weapons development, force deployment, and arms control negotiations. That must be our goal.

Let me repeat the elements of our present nuclear position:

- NATO's current military strategy calls for early use of nuclear weapons in response to a Soviet conventional attack.
- The war plans to carry out such a nuclear strategy are in the hands of NATO troop commanders.
- Twenty-five thousand nuclear warheads have been de-

ployed and stockpiled at sea and on land to be used in accordance with these war plans.

And yet, in this situation, no human mind has conceived of how to initiate the use of nuclear weapons with benefit to the initiator.

As I pointed out earlier, not only are more and more political and military leaders coming to share this point of view, but more and more are expressing it publicly. Lord Carver, the retired Chief of the British Defence Staff, put it forcefully in the statement I quoted in Chapter 4: "Any nuclear exchange, however limited it might be, is bound to leave NATO worse off in comparison to the Warsaw Pact . . . [therefore] to initiate use of nuclear weapons . . . seems to me to be criminally irresponsible."

Most Americans are simply unaware that NATO strategy calls for early initiation of the use of nuclear weapons in a conflict with the Soviets. Eighty percent of them believe we would not use such weapons unless the Soviets used them first. They would be shocked to learn they are mistaken. And they would be horrified to be told that senior military commanders themselves believe that to carry out our present strategy would lead to the destruction of our society.

But those are the facts.

It is true that some civilian "experts" consider the damage resulting from a nuclear exchange would be tolerable.

- In the fall of 1981, a deputy undersecretary of defense said: "Dig a hole, cover it with a couple of doors and then throw three feet of dirt on top. . . . If there are enough shovels to go around everybody's going to make it. . . . Recovery times could be two to four years."
- In the same year, the director of the Arms Control and

Disarmament Agency said, "Japan, after all, not only survived but flourished after the nuclear attack."

- A few months later the executive director of the General Advisory Committee on Arms Control and Disarmament said: "I think it is possible to survive a nuclear war. . . . Nuclear war is a destructive thing, but it is still in large part a physics problem. . . . Hiroshima, after it was bombed, was back and operating three days later."

And in 1980 Vice President Bush, when discussing how to win a nuclear exchange, said that one side could win such a war if "you have a survivability of command and control, survivability of industrial potential, protection of a percentage of your citizens, and you have a capability that inflicts more damage on the opposition than it can inflict on you. That's the way you can have a winner."*

But as one who has confronted the possibility of nuclear exchanges, I find such comments incomprehensible. And I believe the majority of the American people do as well. McGeorge Bundy had such views in mind when he wrote:

Think-tank analysts can set levels of acceptable damage well up in the tens of millions of lives. They can assume that the loss of dozens of great cities is somehow a real choice for sane men. They are in an unreal world. In the real world of real political leaders—whether here or in the Soviet Union—a decision that would bring even one hy-

---

*Statements such as these drew adverse comments from critics. We therefore hear fewer of them today. But the Pentagon's strategic planning, weapons development, and arms procurement continue to be driven by a determination to maintain dominance at each stage of a nuclear conflict, which it is assumed could last for days or weeks until one side or the other prevailed.

drogen bomb on one city of one's own country would be recognized in advance as a catastrophic blunder; ten bombs on ten cities would be a disaster beyond history; and a hundred bombs on a hundred cities are unthinkable.

The fact is, the Emperor has no clothes. Our present nuclear policy is bankrupt.

And yet today we are poised, ready to leap forward in a new series of escalatory moves that will lead inexorably to still greater instability and still greater risk of catastrophe for all humanity. President Reagan's intuitive reaction that we must change course—that we must recognize nuclear warheads cannot be used as military weapons—is correct. To continue as in the past would be totally irresponsible. It would be, as the Catholic bishops and other religious leaders have emphasized, morally wrong.

How long will it take for us to recognize this fact?

As I write these words, the fragmentary reports of the effects of the Chernobyl reactor failure continue to shock the world:

- Children and pregnant women in Poland were exposed to absorption of radioactive iodine in their thyroid glands.
- Much of Sweden's population was subjected to radioactive fallout, and a small but measurable increase in cancer-related deaths is projected over the next forty-five years.
- Fifty thousand to a hundred thousand Soviet citizens may face long-term health problems.
- Contaminated farm produce in many of the surrounding countries has been destroyed. The 1986 crops from hundreds of square miles of farmland in the Ukraine are

likely to be lost. And an as yet undetermined area of agricultural land in the region of the accident may be unusable for years.

But, as Professor Everett Mendelsohn, a Harvard science historian, has pointed out, "The radiation from the Chernobyl reactor accident is minuscule [compared] to what we would face in a nuclear war." Can we not use Chernobyl to help us visualize more clearly the horrors of nuclear war and thus move more quickly to reduce the risk of such a disaster?

Let me unequivocally restate my own views.

Having spent seven years as Secretary of Defense dealing with the problems unleashed by the initial nuclear chain reaction forty-three years ago, I do not believe we can avoid the serious and unacceptable risk of nuclear war until we recognize —and until we base all our military plans, defense budgets, weapons deployments, and arms negotiations on the recognition—that nuclear weapons serve no military purpose whatsoever. They are totally useless—except to deter one's opponent from using them.

This is my view today. It was my view in the early 1960s.

At that time, in long private conversations with successive Presidents—Kennedy and Johnson—I recommended, without qualification, that they never initiate, under any circumstances, the use of nuclear weapons. I believe they accepted my recommendations.

I am not suggesting that all U.S. Presidents would behave as I believe Presidents Kennedy and Johnson would have, although I hope they would. But I do wish to suggest that if we are to reach a consensus within the Alliance on the military role of nuclear weapons—an issue that is fundamental to the peace and security of both the West and the East—we must face and answer the following questions:

- Can we conceive of ways to utilize nuclear weapons, in response to Soviet aggression with conventional forces, which would be beneficial to NATO?
- Would any U.S. President be likely to authorize such use of nuclear weapons?
- If we cannot conceive of a beneficial use of nuclear weapons, and if we believe it unlikely that a U.S. President would authorize their use in such a situation, should we continue to accept the risks associated with basing NATO's strategy, war plans, and nuclear warhead deployment on the assumption that the weapons would be used in the early hours of an East-West conflict?
- Would the types of conventional forces recommended by General Rogers, Professor William Kaufmann, the European Security Study, and others serve as an adequate deterrent to nonnuclear aggression by the USSR? If so, are we not acting irresponsibly by continuing to accept the increased risks of nuclear war associated with present NATO strategy in place of the modest expenditures necessary to acquire and sustain such forces?
- Do we favor a world free of nuclear weapons? If so, should we not recognize that such a world would not provide a "nuclear deterrent" to Soviet conventional aggression? If we could live without such a deterrent then, why can't we do so now—thereby taking a large step toward a nonnuclear world?

In sum, to reduce the risk of blundering into disaster, I propose we adopt the view that the military role of nuclear weapons is limited to deterrence of one's opponent's use of such weapons, and that we move as rapidly as an Alliance consensus can be formed—it is likely to evolve gradually over the next five or ten years—to base all our military plans, our defense budgets, our weapons development and deployment programs, and our arms negotiations on that proposition.

I realize I am proposing a radical change in attitude toward NATO's present nuclear strategy. And I realize, too, that attitudes will not change quickly. They are based both on deep-seated feelings of mistrust of the Soviet Union and on misperceptions of how nuclear weapons can protect us against Soviet aggression.

In Chapter 1, I described three crises from my own term as Secretary of Defense: Soviet pressure on Berlin in 1961; the introduction of missiles into Cuba in 1962; and the Middle East War in 1967. My purpose was to provide a personal perspective on one of the central themes of this book: things can go wrong. Actions can lead to unintended consequences. Signals can be misread. Technologies can fail. Crises can escalate even if neither side wants war.

Three recent events—the Soviet shoot-down of Korean Air Lines Flight 007, leading to the death of 269 civilians; the explosion of the U.S. space shuttle *Challenger;* and the nuclear reactor accident at Chernobyl—reinforce this point and serve to remind us all how often we are the victims of misinformation, mistaken judgments, and human fallibility. It is inconceivable to me that in a crisis situation, with all its inevitable pressures, decisions regarding the use of nuclear weapons would be unaffected by such factors.

The loss of KAL 007 was a great tragedy. But a similar error in judgment leading to the launch of nuclear weapons would be an unparalleled disaster. We must act to avoid such a disaster by making less and less likely the use of these weapons. Our present course is taking us precisely in the opposite direction.

A U.S. security expert, predicting that an arms control

agreement limiting strategic nuclear arms was unlikely in the near term, recently forecast that without such a limitation the number of Soviet strategic warheads would more than double to approximately twenty-four thousand. At least one-half of the greatly expanded force would be targeted on "time-urgent" targets, thereby increasing U.S. first-strike fears and reducing crisis stability.

The majority of security experts in the West continue to assert that nuclear weapons and the threat of their first use are essential to our defense. While I totally disagree with that view, I do recognize that unity within the Alliance is the foundation of our strength. We must, therefore, recognize that major changes in nuclear strategy are unlikely until they receive broad support both from the American people and from the other members of NATO as well. That is why we should begin immediately to build that support. The purpose of this book is to contribute to that process.

We should begin by discussing openly and candidly, in public forums throughout the NATO countries, the risks of the nuclear world we live in. Those discussions could be followed by a series of actions by governments, which, over a period of years, would lead to the new long-term strategy and force goals. The initial steps could include: acceptance of General Bernard Rogers's proposal to strengthen NATO's conventional forces,* thereby permitting an early shift to a strategy of "no early first use"; a sharp acceleration in the reduction and redeployment of tactical weapons in Europe; a restructuring of the Strategic Defense Initiative to clearly limit it to a research program; and negotiations with the Soviets designed both to strengthen the

---

*With NATO's population 65 percent greater than that of the Warsaw Pact and its gross national product 200 percent larger, NATO is clearly capable, both politically and financially, of strengthening its conventional forces if such action would reduce the risk of nuclear war.

ABM Treaty and to achieve sharp reductions in strategic offensive arms.

Chernobyl will serve to magnify the justified concern of the nonaligned and neutral nations over the behavior of the superpowers and their allies. One need not accept fully the thesis of nuclear winter to recognize that a nuclear exchange between East and West would bring widespread destruction to the peoples of the rest of the world. They therefore can be expected to demand a voice in those decisions of the superpowers that affect the risk of war: a voice in arms-control decisions; a voice in the formulation of nuclear strategy; and a voice in the development of nuclear force levels.

The Chancellor of the Federal Republic of Germany feels justified in demanding reparations from the USSR for damages suffered by his country from the Chernobyl accident. If such a demand is warranted, then surely the governments of India, Brazil, and Sweden, for example, would be justified in demanding that they be informed of the risks to which the nuclear weapons programs of the superpowers are exposing them, and of the actions—if any—that the superpowers will take in order to reduce those risks.

The arms negotiations now underway in Geneva represent a historic opportunity to change course and to take the first step toward the long-term goals I have proposed. We can lay the foundation for entering the twenty-first century with a totally different nuclear strategy, one of mutual security instead of war-fighting; with vastly smaller nuclear forces, no more than one thousand weapons in place of fifty thousand; and with a dramatically lower risk that our civilization will be destroyed.

Several themes should govern our attitudes and policies as we move through those negotiations toward our long-term objectives.

Each side must recognize that neither will permit the other

to achieve a meaningful superiority. Attempts to gain such an advantage are not only futile but dangerous.

The forces pushing each side in the direction of a first-strike posture—whether real or perceived—must be reversed. A stable balance at the lowest possible level should be the goal.

Our technological edge should be exploited vigorously to enhance our security, but in a manner that does not threaten the stability of deterrence. Space surveillance and data processing, which form a large portion of the SDI program, illustrate what technology could contribute to treaty verification.

We must not forget Winston Churchill's warning that "the Stone Age may return on the gleaming wings of science." We must shed the fatalistic belief that new technologies, no matter how threatening, cannot be stopped. While laboratory research cannot be constrained by verifiable agreement, technology itself provides increasingly powerful tools that can be used to impede development and to stop deployment. Only an absence of political will, for example, hinders a verifiable agreement preventing the deployment of more-threatening ballistic missiles, since they require many observable flight tests prior to deployment.

We must also allay legitimate fears on both sides: Soviet fear of our technology, and our fear of their obsessive secrecy. These apprehensions provide an opportunity for a bargain: Soviet acceptance of more-intrusive verification in return for American constraints on applications of its technological innovation. Penetration of Soviet secrecy is to our mutual advantage, even if the Kremlin does not yet understand that. So is technological restraint, even though it runs against the American grain.

We have reached the present dangerous and absurd confrontation by a long series of steps, many of which seemed to be rational in their time. Step by step, we can undo much of the damage.

The program sketched in this volume would, I believe, initiate that process. But whether or not there is acceptance of my specific proposals, we can surely agree on this: we must develop a national consensus for a long-term strategy for the second half century of the nuclear age—a strategy that will reduce the unacceptable risks we now face and begin to restore confidence in the future.

Is not our first duty and obligation to assure, beyond doubt, the survival of our civilization?

Appendixes

Glossary
Notes
Acknowledgments
Index

I. U.S. AND SOVIET STRATEGIC WARHEADS

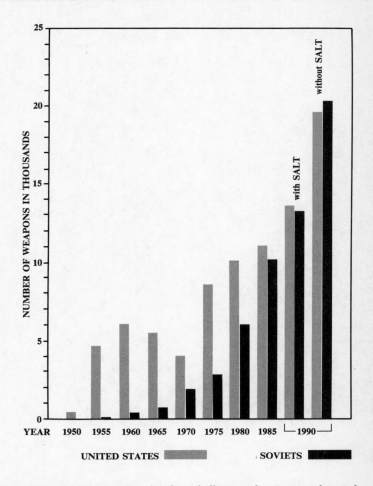

The chart shows strategic warheads on ballistic and cruise missiles, and on long-range bombers. It indicates that the number of warheads in the U.S. and Soviet arsenals has grown steadily, but increased sharply after each began MIRVing their missiles in the 1970s.

II. THE TECHNOLOGY RACE

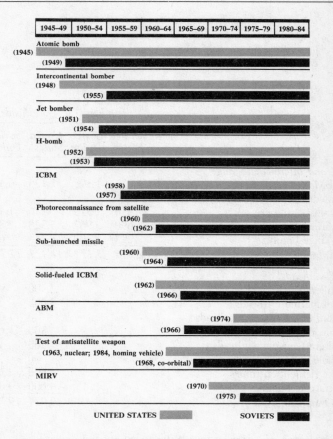

For each innovation in military technology, two lines are shown to represent when each of the superpowers tested or deployed the innovation. As the chart shows, each innovation is quickly matched.

SOURCE: Philip Morrison, "After Trinity: Insecurity Through Technical Prowess," in Union of Concerned Scientists, *Toward a New Security: Lessons of the Forty Years Since Trinity* (Washington, D.C.: Union of Concerned Scientists, 1983), p. 22.

III. U.S. AND SOVIET NUCLEAR ARSENALS IN 1985

	Missiles or bombers		Warheads	
	United States	Soviet Union	United States	Soviet Union
Long- and intermediate-range				
ICBMs	1,023	1,398	2,126	6,420
Intermediate- range missiles (land-based ballistic and cruise)	236	514	236	1,435
Submarine- launched ballistic	690	967	5,728	2,887
Long-range bombers	297	300	3,334	600
Subtotal	*2,246*	*3,179*	*11,424*	*11,342*
Other warheads				
Artillery shells			2,400	900
Antisubmarine warheads			2,000	600
Antiship cruise missile warheads			0	1,000
Battlefield ballistic missile warheads			300	1,600
Antiaircraft missile warheads			200	300
Antiballistic missile warheads			0	32
Atomic demolition mines			600	some
Nonstrategic bombs			4,000	4,000
*Overall total warheads**			*20,924*	*19,774*

*Not including reloads or warheads stockpiled but not deployed.

SOURCES: For strategic weapons: U.S. Department of Defense, *Soviet Military Power, 1984* (Washington, D.C.: GPO, 1984), pp. 24, 26; U.S. Department of Defense, *Report of the Secretary of Defense, Caspar W. Weinberger, to the Congress, 1986* (Washington, D.C.: GPO, 1985), Chart III.E.4 and Appendix C. For U.S. forces, we assume ten warheads per Poseidon, eight per Trident I, eight bombs and short-range attack missiles on all 241 B-52G/Hs and six on each of the 56 FB-111s, and twelve air-launched cruise missiles on each of the ninety B-52G bombers. For Soviet forces, we assume four warheads per SS-17, ten per SS-18, 6 per SS-19, seven per SS-N-18, nine per SS-N-20. We do not include Soviet bombers assigned to naval aviation, and we assume an average of two bombs and/or attack missiles per bomber, based on Senate Committee on Armed Forces, *Department of Defense Authorizations for Appropriations for FY 1985: Hearings,* 98th Cong., 2d sess., February 1, 1984, p. 123.

For intermediate-range missiles: Arms Control Association from U.S. government data.

For other nuclear weapons: Nuclear Weapons Databook Staff, in *World Armaments and Disarmament SIPRI Yearbook, 1985* (London: Taylor & Francis, 1985).

Chart based on one in Harold A. Feiveson, Richard H. Ullman, and Frank von Hippel, "Reducing U.S. and Soviet Nuclear Arsenals," *Bulletin of the Atomic Scientists,* August 1985, p. 146.

IV. GROWTH OF U.S. AND SOVIET STRATEGIC NUCLEAR MISSILE AND BOMBER FORCES, 1945–1990

	1945	1950	1955	1960	1965
WARHEADS					
U.S.					
Missiles				68	1,050
Bombs & ALCMs	2	450	4,750	6,000	4,500
Total	2	450	4,750	6,068	5,550
Soviet					
Missiles				some	225
Bombs & ALCMs			20	300	375
Total			20	300	600
DELIVERY SYSTEMS					
U.S.					
Bombers		some	400	600	600
ICBMs				20	850
SLBMs				48	400
ALCMs					
Soviet					
Bombers			some	150	250
ICBMs				some	200
SLBMs				15	25
ALCMs					

Excludes intermediate-range missiles and carrier-based and theater bomber forces. Does not include the Soviet Backfire bomber.

*The first column for 1990 assumes U.S. and Soviet forces are constrained by SALT II. The second column assumes aggressive modernization without SALT constraints.

	1970	1975	1980	1985	1990a*	1990b*
WARHEADS						
U.S.						
Missiles	1,800	6,100	7,300	7,900	8,240	10,580
Bombs & ALCMs	2,200	2,400	2,800	3,300	5,376	8,196
Total	*4,000*	*8,500*	*10,100*	*11,200*	*13,616*	*18,776*
Soviet						
Missiles	1,600	2,500	5,500	9,300	10,892	16,886
Bombs & ALCMs	200	300	500	600	2,400	3,440
Total	*1,800*	*2,800*	*6,000*	*9,900*	*13,292*	*20,326*
DELIVERY SYSTEMS						
U.S.						
Bombers	550	400	340	263	319	428
ICBMs	1,054	1,054	1,050	1,028	1,000	1,160
SLBMs	656	656	656	648	640	784
ALCMs				1,080	1,760	2,648
Soviet						
Bombers	145	135	156	160	225	328
ICBMs	1,300	1,527	1,398	1,398	1,398	1,954
SLBMs	300	784	1,028	924	948	974
ALCMs				200	1,380	1,772

SOURCES: *The Military Balance 1983–84* by the International Institute for Strategic Studies; DOD Annual Report for FY '82; JCS Posture Statement for FY '86. Data for 1990 are from the Congressional Research Service Report No. 84—174F, October 5, 1984.

V. THE STAR WARS DEFENSE SYSTEM: A Technical Note*

For more than a quarter of a century the United States has carried on research programs aimed at devising the means to destroy Soviet missiles before they reach their targets. Since the mid-1960s we have known how to shoot down a small percentage of the incoming missiles. The Strategic Defense Initiative (SDI), or Star Wars program, through a vastly expanded research effort, seeks to so increase the "kill" capability of an antiballistic missile system as to justify its deployment.

As I noted in Chapter 4, President Reagan and Secretary of Defense Caspar Weinberger have suggested on numerous occasions that SDI is aimed at developing a system that would fully protect our population. However, it is generally accepted by the technicians supervising the program that such a leakproof defense is not a realistic goal for at least four or five decades, if ever. Therefore, current research is directed toward a system which, while not perfect, would be sufficiently effective to provide partial protection to our urban populations. Defense of hardened targets such as missile silos and command centers would be far simpler to devise, but the Administration on several occasions has stated that this is not the goal of Star Wars.

*This appendix is intended to give the interested layman a brief description of the antiballistic missile technology being developed under the SDI. The program has not advanced to the stage where final judgment can be expressed as to its technical feasibility; however, experts in the field are beginning to comment on the system's potential, and I have included some of their comments. I am neither a scientist nor an engineer. Therefore, this statement is not original with me. It has been drawn from the articles listed at the end of the Notes section.

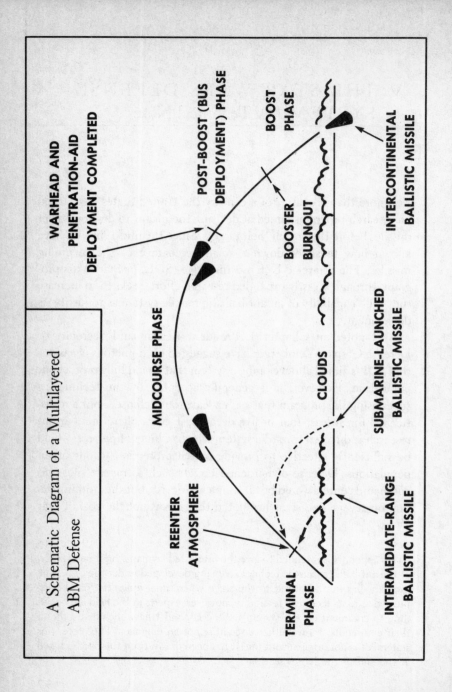

A Schematic Diagram of a Multilayered ABM Defense

WARHEAD AND PENETRATION-AID DEPLOYMENT COMPLETED

POST-BOOST (BUS DEPLOYMENT) PHASE

BOOST PHASE

INTERCONTINENTAL BALLISTIC MISSILE

BOOSTER BURNOUT

MIDCOURSE PHASE

REENTER ATMOSPHERE

CLOUDS

SUBMARINE-LAUNCHED BALLISTIC MISSILE

TERMINAL PHASE

INTERMEDIATE-RANGE BALLISTIC MISSILE

The SDI, as now planned, envisions an antimissile system composed of four to seven "layers." The goal is to detect and intercept ballistic missiles in each of the stages of their flight from silos in the Soviet Union and submarines at sea to targets in the United States and Western Europe.

There are four flight stages. In the boost phase the missile is launched and its booster rocket burns. The boost phase for existing ballistic missiles ranges from three to five minutes. In the postboost phase, which lasts from two to ten minutes, a postboost vehicle (also called a bus) separates from the burned-out booster rocket and proceeds to release warheads—more than one for MIRVed missiles—and various "penetration aids" designed to fool the SDI system. In the midcourse phase, the warheads and penetration aids travel on a ballistic flight trajectory through space. Land-based intercontinental ballistic missiles require fifteen to twenty-five minutes to complete this phase of flight, while submarine launched missiles need from five to twenty minutes. Finally, missiles enter the terminal stage of flight, in which they reenter the atmosphere and, in about one minute, descend upon cities and military targets.

Can a system to shoot down missiles in each of these stages be built and made effective with foreseeable technologies?

Discussion of the technical prospects for an SDI system requires much speculation, but both proponents and opponents of the plan recognize that constructing and maintaining the system would represent the most complex technical task ever undertaken in human history.

To make Star Wars work will require successful development of a great number of subsystems. These would have to quickly detect a Soviet missile attack, track each missile and warhead in the various stages of flight, discriminate them from decoys, and destroy them. SDI command and control systems would have to be capable of coordinating human and computer decision-making. And since humans could not adequately direct the effort to destroy attacking missiles, computer hardware and software would have to provide "battle management" sufficient to coordinate the various layers of attack.

Major parts of the system would be based in space. For this we would need to build hundreds or thousands of satellites, develop adequate power sources for them, and lift them into outer space. We would need to construct thousands more sea-, air-, and ground-based missile interceptors and sensors.

But such a description does not do full justice to the magnitude of the task. The SDI has been compared to a challenge initiated by President Kennedy: putting a man on the moon. But there is a fundamental difference between the two tasks: the moon didn't fight back. The Soviet Union, on the other hand, has indicated that it will respond vigorously if we endeavor to render impotent its missile arsenal. It will attempt to overwhelm, evade, or directly attack our SDI systems.

Lieutenant General James Abrahamson, SDI's director, has recognized that the response of Soviet planners to SDI will be to try to defeat the system. Thus, SDI will have to be effective against existing and projected countermeasures in order to achieve its aim. Abrahamson flatly predicts such an outcome: "The large number of opportunities to engage the threat with [a multilayered] architecture leads to an expectation of achieving very low levels of defense leakage even if the enemy proliferates his offensive forces in response to our defense."

But ensuring an effective SDI system in the face of Soviet countermeasures would be a daunting task. The most obvious Soviet response would be to increase the number of missiles and the number of warheads carried by those missiles. The Soviets already possess more than 2,300 long-range ballistic missiles with some 9,500 warheads. But SDI cannot assume it will face only those numbers. In the absence of arms control limitations, for example, the Soviets might be able to put up to 30 warheads on its 308 SS-18 missiles, which now carry no more than 10 warheads. Experts in the SDI organization have estimated that the Soviets could deploy 30,000 to 40,000 ballistic missile warheads by the end of the century.

Numerically increasing the Soviet arsenal is only the first countermeasure to consider. There are far cheaper ways to defeat an SDI system. Both we and the Soviets are currently engaged in efforts to develop various types of penetration aids to ensure that missiles will reach their targets. As we survey the technologies under consideration for SDI, I will point out some of the countermeasures that could be developed to try to defeat them.

According to Abrahamson, "the most important" layer of the SDI system is the one that will attack missiles in their boost phase. The reason why is clear: it is in the boost phase that the Soviet missile arsenal is at its most vulnerable. Booster rockets are easier to detect and track than postboost vehicles or warheads because they emit strong infrared radiation. Boosters are also larger and more fragile and thus easier to destroy. In addition, because each booster can carry multiple warheads and penetration aids, more of the Soviet arsenal can be "killed" with less shots in the boost phase.

Boost-phase defenses face a fundamental obstacle, however: where do we deploy them? The two alternatives are to station them on satellites in outer space or to "pop them up" into space from submarines once an attack has commenced. However, neither option appears feasible in light of potential countermeasures.

As the Fletcher panel, charged by the President with laying the technical groundwork for the SDI, noted in their 1983 study, "Survivability is potentially a serious problem for the space-based components." Satellites carrying SDI sensors and interceptors would be vulnerable to attack by an array of Soviet antisatellite weapons, including nuclear space mines, homing kill vehicles, and lasers. In fact, as Administration officials acknowledge, the same technologies used for antimissile weapons could produce potent antisatellite weapons. And satellites, moving in predictable orbits, are easier to target than missiles. The department manager for systems analysis at the Sandia Laboratories said in 1985: "I think boost phase [defense] may be out of the question, which is unfortunate. . . . Every time we look at it, it seems very difficult to ensure the survivability of space-based assets." Because of the criticality of an effective boost-phase layer to the overall performance of the SDI defense, the opponent might need only to punch a hole in the boost-phase layer to severely degrade the defense.

In response to the Soviet antisatellite threat, we would have to develop counter-countermeasures. We could attempt to harden our satellites against enemy blows, but such hardening would increase the weight of our systems and thus increase the cost of lifting them into space. Moreover, nuclear explosions from Soviet space mines could probably wreck our satellites, hardened or not. We could increase the number of satellites, attempt to disguise them, or give them the capability to maneuver away from enemy fire. Such efforts would create an endless and expensive cat-and-mouse game with the Soviets. We could also use the kill mechanisms—designed to shoot down Soviet missiles—to attack their hostile satellites. But this would not only magnify our weapons and battle management needs, it would also create the possibility of a preemptive strike in space: If war seemed inevitable, whoever shot first would gain a significant advantage.

The other option for the boost phase is to deploy "pop-up" weapons on submarine- and land-based missiles. But most weapons under consideration for boost-phase intercept would be too heavy to be popped up. The only viable candidate for a pop-up role is a concept called the X-ray laser, a so-called directed energy weapon. Directed-energy weapons—lasers or particle beams—create beams of energy made of a single wavelength of radiation, or of electrically neutral atoms, respectively.

The X-ray laser would focus X-rays from a nuclear bomb explosion into powerful beams of directed energy. When Soviet missiles were launched, hundreds of these weapons would be popped up. As the weapons rose into outer space, they would track the missiles. The nuclear bombs would explode, produce X-ray beams focused on the booster, whose impact would create a shock wave in its skin and destroy the missile.

In order to reach Soviet missiles in space in time to destroy them, the X-ray would have to be launched almost simultaneously with Soviet missiles. Human decision-making would thus be impossible; computers would have to give the order to fire.

Moreover, a single countermeasure—one that appears quite feasible—would decisively defeat the X-ray laser. The Soviets could develop "fast-burn" booster rockets that could burn out and release the postboost vehicle in far less than the three minutes required by current missiles. Indeed, the Fletcher panel stated that fast-burn boosters could allow the missile to complete the boost phase in one minute—before it had left the atmosphere to enter outer space. Not only would pop-up systems be unable to reach their targets with such speed; X-rays simply cannot penetrate the atmosphere.

Even a more modest reduction in boost time would cause problems for the X-ray laser. If we wanted the weapons to get a good shot at Soviet missiles in boost phase, they would have to be launched from submarines patrolling close to Soviet shores, where they might be vulnerable to Soviet attack, or on the territories of such Soviet neighbors as Turkey or China, who might not be amenable to such an arrangement. But such positioning would be necessary because the earth is round: only if the X-ray laser was launched near Soviet silo fields would it have a clear line of fire against boosters. The Pentagon has stated that a Soviet fast-burn booster—which appears feasible without drastically altering missile weight or performance—"would cast doubts" on the effectiveness of the X-ray laser for boost-phase defense.

These weaknesses in the X-ray laser concept have forced SDI officials to place their hopes for boost-phase intercept in space-based systems despite their vulnerability. The primary candidate now is a kinetic-energy weapon: a mechanism that fires at high speed a projectile (a bullet or rocket) that would simply ram into the enemy missile or warhead. The weapon, called the space-based kinetic kill vehicle, is based on less exotic technologies than many other SDI concepts. It is envisioned that perhaps five thousand of these chemical-fueled rockets would be deployed on thousands of satellites.

At least that many satellites would be required to compensate for the so-called absentee problem. To explain briefly, the kinetic-energy rockets, relatively slow and with limited range, would have to be placed in low orbits in order to reach launched Soviet boosters in time. But objects in low orbits revolve around the earth quickly—more quickly than the earth rotates on its axis—and thus cannot remain over Soviet missile-launch areas continuously. Therefore, a large number of satellites would be required to ensure that enough of their relatively short-range rockets would be within reach of Soviet missiles at all times.

Fast-burn boosters, which would negate the X-ray laser as a boost-phase weapon, would also pose severe problems for the kinetic vehicle. As I noted above, fast-burn rockets could finish their boost phase in the atmosphere. Kinetic vehicles are unlikely to perform effectively in the atmosphere, because atmospheric friction could interfere with their homing mechanisms. In fact, the kinetic vehicles, far slower than laser weapons or other directed-energy weapons, would have trouble reaching enough of even existing types of booster rockets before they burned out.

Former Secretary of Defense Harold Brown has stated that the concept of the kinetic-kill vehicle is "unpromising" because of the feasibility of effective countermeasures. Although the kinetic vehicle is being pushed as a major component not only of the boost-phase layer but also for destruction of warheads in later stages of flight, even its proponents acknowledge that the weight of the kinetic vehicle must be dramatically reduced if the system is to be feasible financially.

The prospects for other kinetic-energy weapons are even more remote. For example, the electromagnetic railgun, which would accelerate small homing projectiles at high speed, would require huge amounts of energy, and placing sufficient energy sources in space would incur huge lift requirements. The program has already encountered considerable technical problems.

Another directed-energy concept, the space-based chemical laser, was once considered promising but now has been deemphasized by the SDI. The chemical laser, like the X-ray laser, would use a concentrated beam of light to burn into the skin of the booster. However, because the chemical laser would lack the power of the X-ray laser, in order to provide sufficient heat to burn the booster, the beam, which would be up to thirty-five hundred miles from its target, would have to focus on the same point on the missile for several seconds while the missile moved at ten thousand miles per hour. In 1983 testimony to Congress, an Air Force major general provided an analogy to this task: "You want to be able to point from the Washington Monument to a baseball on the top of the Empire State Building and hold it there while both of you are moving." He concluded, "As a technologist, I view the whole thing with a fair amount of trepidation."

The space-based laser would suffer the same absentee problem facing the kinetic-kill vehicle, since its beams would not be powerful enough to reach targets from high orbit. Since only those satellites "on station" over missiles at the time of attack could respond, each satellite would have to destroy a large number of boosters and thus would have to be enormously powerful. But such a requirement suggests a need for launching extremely heavy power supplies into space.

Another laser concept, the ground-based free-electron laser, is now considered a more viable concept by the SDI organization for both boost- and postboost-phase intercept. Under this scheme, ground-based laser systems would shoot beams through the atmosphere and into outer space, where the beams would bounce off orbiting mirrors and hit attacking missiles and warheads.

Keeping the laser on the ground would eliminate the problem of lifting large power sources into space, but the free-electron laser concept presents another set of problems. The first is to develop lasers ten thousand times brighter than any existing laser. A second is to ensure that the laser beams can remain focused on their path through the atmosphere and into space. While advances have been made in this area, the problem has by no means been solved. A third problem is that clouds could block the beams, and thus a large number of widely dispersed laser stations might be required to provide a high likelihood that, in the event of attack, a sufficient number of stations would have clear skies above. Finally, space-based mirrors would face the same absentee problem confronting space-based interceptor weapons.

Moreover, one can envision various countermeasures that would undermine the effectiveness of the free-electron laser and other so-called optical lasers (such as the chemical laser). The Soviets could develop boosters that would rotate as they ascended. Since optical lasers must focus on a single point for several seconds in order to burn a hole in the booster's skin, such rotation could prevent its destruction. The Soviets could also coat each missile with an ablative shield that would absorb the heat and evaporate but leave the booster intact. In addition, fast-burn boosters would pose severe problems for optical lasers.

But perhaps the most serious problem concerns the space-based mirrors. These would be even more vulnerable than the orbiting battle stations envisioned by other SDI concepts. Such mirrors would have to be three or four times larger than any mirror ever constructed, and they could be ruined by collision with small pellets released by the Soviets.

Moving beyond the boost and post-boost phases, the SDI envisions three or four types of high-speed ground-based kinetic-energy missiles for interception of warheads in the midcourse and terminal portions of the flight. A concept called Braduskill, which would employ heat-seeking and radar guidance, is a candidate for midcourse intercept. Another type of weapon would shoot down missiles just prior to their reentry into the atmosphere, while two others would destroy them after reentry. These terminal systems would use heat-seeking guidance.

Because the "footprint"—the area over which each rocket would provide protection—would be relatively small, a highly effective SDI defense would require perhaps thousands of ground-based rocket sites across the United States and Europe. A great deal of land would be required, especially in densely populated Western Europe, which would face an array of shorter-range ballistic missiles that would not be easily engaged in earlier stages of flight.

Moreover, terminal defenses would face significant countermeasures in their effort to defend vulnerable civilian targets from the vast destructive power of nuclear weapons. The Soviets could "sal-

vage-fuse" their warheads, so that they would explode in the atmosphere upon sensing or colliding with our interceptors—exploding
with sufficient power to destroy urban populations. In addition, the
Soviets could develop a maneuvering reentry vehicle (MARV) with
small fins or specially configured noses that would allow the reentry
vehicle to veer away from its apparent target and toward another
target and thus evade the defenses. To counter MARVs we might
have to arm our kinetic rockets with nuclear warheads whose explosive power could destroy Soviet reentry vehicles without a head-
on collision. Thus, the final stage of the SDI defense could involve
the detonation of hundreds of U.S. nuclear warheads above our
country.

Despite the many difficulties with these various schemes for destroying missiles, such a task only represents one component of the
challenge facing SDI. Before we can destroy Soviet weapons, we will
have to track them along their flight paths and discriminate between
actual warheads and the various decoys released by the postboost
vehicle. As in the case of kill mechanisms, every concept for tracking
and discriminating suggests another countermeasure.

The first layer of SDI's detection system might be about a dozen
satellites—in geosynchronous orbit (matching the earth's rotation)
—capable of detecting the infrared emissions from Soviet booster
rockets. This Boost Surveillance and Tracking System would trans-
mit the warning of attack to the next level of sensors, the Space
Surveillance and Tracking System (SSTS), deployed on some one
hundred to two hundred satellites in low orbit. The task of identifying the attacking missiles would be made more difficult if the Soviets
constructed dummy missile silos and fake boosters that could approximate the infrared signatures of actual missile-carrying rockets. SSTS
would track missiles and warheads from the boost phase through the
midcourse stage of flight. Sensing in the late midcourse phase could
be augmented by the Airborne Optical System, a fleet of aircraft
with on-board infrared detectors.

But Soviet explosion of nuclear bombs in space would pose major
problems for detection of infrared signatures. Such explosions could

cripple sensors or emit enough infrared radiation to blind them. SDI technicians are concentrating much effort on "hardening" sensors against explosions and making them capable of sensing in a nuclear environment.

However, as SDI officials recognize, the reading of infrared signals, so-called passive discrimination, will be insufficient for the task of identifying warheads in the long midcourse phase. Warheads emit far less infrared radiation than boosters and are difficult to locate in the darkness of space. But the task becomes far more daunting in the face of likely Soviet countermeasures: loading up its missiles with additional warheads and myriad penetration aids.

As I noted above, the heaviest Soviet missiles could carry up to thirty warheads. The congressional Office of Technology Assessment estimates that the Soviets could deploy on its missiles some ten lightweight decoys for each warhead. Decoys could be balloonlike objects or pieces of metal or plastic. Thus, midcourse sensors might have to track hundreds of thousands of objects. The release of additional penetration aids such as chaff (fragments of metal wire) and aerosol clouds would further increase the challenge facing SDI. Discrimination of warheads from decoys would be especially difficult in the vacuum of outer space, since without the effects of "atmospheric drag," genuine and phony warheads would glide along in seemingly identical trajectories. And the Soviets could disguise their warheads to make them appear like balloon decoys.

Thus, the SDI organization is developing a concept called interactive discrimination: using beams of energy to produce observable distinctions between warheads and decoys. Gentle taps from free-electron lasers—the same weapons that might be used for destroying missiles—could induce vibrations in the warheads that might be distinguishable from those of decoys.

Another type of directed-energy weapon, the neutral-particle beam, which was considered but largely rejected as a kill mechanism, is now the SDI organization's preferred concept for interactive discrimination. In such a system, streams of neutral hydrogen atoms would be pushed into a particle accelerator and forced out as narrow beams of energy. For interactive discrimination the beams would irradiate the various warheads and decoys, and the warheads would give off distinctive radiation.

It is no accident that particle beams have essentially been rejected as a kill mechanism: the concept poses major problems that might also preclude its effectiveness as a sensing system. Particle-beam systems would require placing large, bulky, accelerators with huge power requirements on vulnerable space satellites.

Technicians have also suggested using small, colliding aerosols and pellets to separate warheads from decoys. But it has yet to be proven that interactive discrimination is a workable concept.

Tracking warheads in the terminal phase would be a less demanding task, since atmospheric drag would facilitate discrimination between reentry vehicles and decoys. But unless the system can perform the crucial task of midcourse discrimination with great effectiveness, there would be far more incoming warheads than the terminal sensors could handle. Moreover, initial Soviet attacks, perhaps with low-flying sea-launched cruise missiles, low-trajectory ballistic missiles, or with the first standard-trajectory ballistic missiles to penetrate the defense, could destroy vulnerable ground-based SDI radars. Various effects of nuclear explosions could blind those sensors even if they were not directly destroyed. The vulnerability of such radars was a prime argument against the Sentinel/Safeguard terminal antiballistic systems the United States developed in the mid-1960s.

Another fundamental task for SDI is developing battle-management and command-and-control systems sufficient to direct thousands of kill weapons at tens of thousands of targets and decoys in an extremely compressed time period and—once the Soviets exploded bombs in the atmosphere and outer space—a nuclear environment. Each layer of missile defense would have to inform the next how well it did in engaging the missile threat and how much of the threat was still traveling toward our territory. The extreme time demands, especially in the boost phase, would leave little room for human intervention, or, as a member of the Fletcher panel put it,

"There is no time for man in the loop." Major advances in artificial intelligence would probably be required to allow computers to perform tasks normally reserved for humans.

Developing and maintaining adequate computer software, according to the Fletcher panel, "will be a task that far exceeds in complexity and difficulty any that has yet been accomplished in the production of civil or military software systems." Two and a half years into the SDI effort, the Pentagon reaffirmed in May 1986 that "the battle management software to be developed for the SDI may be the most complex ever attempted." SDI studies conclude that ten million to a hundred million lines of computer code would be required.

Finally, as the Fletcher panel noted, this fantastically complex software—like the SDI system as a whole—could never be fully tested short of engaging in an actual nuclear war. It would have to work the very first time.

Two additional and related SDI tasks, to which I alluded several times above, are power and space transportation.

As General Abrahamson has acknowledged, "many of the SDI systems in orbit are going to be very power-hungry." To provide sufficient power for the system, the United States would have to develop and perhaps lift into space far more power than has ever been lifted in the past. The heaviest power reactor lifted thus far was a 12-kilowatt source carried in the Skylab program. By contrast, some 10,000 to 1,000,000 kilowatts might be needed to power SDI systems. A current U.S. program, SP-100, is developing a space-based nuclear reactor of 300 kilowatts or more.

Even if we could develop sufficient power sources, we could not take for granted our ability to deploy reactors and other elements of the system in space at manageable cost. SDI lift requirements would not end with the deployment of the system, since space-based systems and mirrors would require periodic maintenance as well as upgrades to deal with new Soviet countermeasures.

Transportation costs would have to be reduced dramatically from present levels. According to a May 1986 Pentagon document, the SDI will require lifting between 20 and 200 million pounds to low earth orbit, and "at today's cost of between $1,000 and $3,000 per pound to orbit, the cost of space transportation alone could approach $60 billion."

The current state of the U.S. space program suggests that it will be difficult to focus on reducing lift costs in the coming decades. The tragedy of the space shuttle *Challenger* and subsequent failures of Titan and Delta boosters suggest long-term problems for both NASA and Air Force space programs. These events also suggest the enormous costs and risks that could be incurred by a program requiring the launch of thousands of military payloads.

The shuttle tragedy—and the Soviet nuclear reactor disaster—should also remind us of human fallibility and of the danger of relying on technology to secure our long-term safety. As I have noted, an SDI system could never be fully tested. Its sensors could misread a nuclear-reactor accident or some other phenomenon on the ground as the beginning of a missile attack and launch SDI interceptors. Some of the weapons might strike Soviet satellites and thus trigger an unintended superpower war. Or the system could massively fail in the event of an actual nuclear attack.

Finally, it is worth repeating that SDI seeks a defense against only one means of delivering nuclear weapons, the ballistic missile. Even an extremely capable Star Wars system would not protect us against a Soviet nuclear attack using bomber aircraft or air- and sea-launched cruise missiles. Mounting defenses against those means of delivery would provide additional technical challenges and costs. Even with such defenses in place, our cities would be vulnerable to nuclear attack by a smuggled suitcase bomb or a giant explosive on a Soviet merchant ship docked in one of our harbors.

Animated Star Wars film sequences may appear like elegant ballets in space. Rockets glide from their silos, only to encounter fine beams of energy from floating satellites. Elsewhere, other light beams are tapping soaring cones, producing tiny quivers. Mirrors spin and reflect beams from the ground. Rockets are lofted out of vast oceans, and aircraft glide toward the heavens to track other flying objects. Rockets rotate as they rise and glide back and forth as they descend, with other rockets rising to embrace them.

What is sometimes forgotten by the observer is that what is being depicted is not some celestial dance, but a nuclear war, one that, even if SDI performs to its full capacity, will cause immense death and destruction on earth.

This is not to say that antiballistic-missile research should not continue. It should. But deployment of any system that such research may produce, at any time in the next several decades, is unlikely to lead to anything other than a rapid acceleration of the arms race.

Glossary

air-launched cruise missile (ALCM): A cruise missile deployed on and launched from an aircraft. See *cruise missile.*

antiballistic missile (ABM): A weapon designed to intercept and destroy attacking nuclear missiles and warheads.

Antiballistic Missile (ABM) Treaty: A treaty signed by the United States and the Soviet Union in 1972 and ratified by the U.S. Senate that prohibits both countries from building nationwide ABM systems or their components; as amended by 1974 Protocol, it allows one limited ABM deployment site and ABM research but bans development, testing, and deployment of space-based systems.

antisatellite weapons (ASAT): A system designed to destroy or disrupt the operation of an adversary's satellites.

assured destruction capability: The capacity to absorb the total weight of an enemy's nuclear strike and retain the capability to launch an attack in a response that would inflict unacceptable damage on the aggressor.

atomic demolition munition (ADM): A nuclear device designed to be emplaced and detonated on or below the ground, or under water; also called a nuclear land mine.

ballistic missile: A rocket designed to propel a nuclear warhead (or warheads) up and through the atmosphere and release it to travel to its target on a free-falling trajectory; includes intercontinental, sea-launched, intermediate-range, and medium-range weapons.

ballistic missile defense (BMD): See *antiballistic missile.*

band of parity: A range of nuclear force levels and types of weapons within which neither side possesses any usable military capability.

battlefield nuclear weapon: See *tactical nuclear weapon.*

command and control: An arrangement of facilities, personnel, procedures, and means of acquiring, processing, and disseminating information to manage military operations.

counterforce: Military plans or weapons directed against an opponent's military forces.

countervalue: Military plans or weapons directed against an opponent's civilian and economic centers.

crisis stability: Confidence shared by adversaries in a crisis that neither side could gain a decisive advantage by using nuclear weapons first; results primarily from the possession by both sides of survivable, secure retaliatory nuclear forces; reduces incentive for a preemptive strike.

cruise missile: A slow-flying pilotless aircraft; difficult to detect by radar; may be armed with nuclear, conventional, or chemical warheads; and may be launched from an aircraft, submarine, surface ship, or land-based platform.

delivery system: Vehicle designed to carry warheads to their targets; includes ballistic and cruise missiles, aircraft, and artillery guns.

demonstration use: The detonation of one or more nuclear weapons in a relatively uninhabited area with no intended direct military effect, the purpose being to display resolve in a conflict.

dual-capable system: A delivery system capable of launching either nuclear or conventional weapons; includes artillery and tactical aircraft.

first strike: Used in the text to refer to what is sometimes called a "disarming first strike": a large nuclear attack intended to destroy the retaliatory forces of the opponent, leaving forces insufficient to inflict substantial damage on the attacker.

first use: The initial use of nuclear weapons of any size and against any target by either party to a conflict.

flexible response: A strategy providing for the maintenance of capabilities to respond in kind or with incrementally greater force to various levels of conventional or nuclear aggression; first proposed to NATO by the United States in 1962; finally adopted by the Alliance in 1967 to replace the strategy of massive retaliation.

follow-on use: Any use of nuclear weapons that follows the initial use of nuclear weapons *by that side.* Compare *second use.*

intercontinental ballistic missile (ICBM): A land-based ballistic missile with a range of approximately 3500 miles or greater. See *ballistic missile.*

intermediate-range ballistic missile (IRBM): A ballistic missile with a range of approximately 1500 to 3500 miles. See *ballistic missile.*

invulnerable retaliatory force: A nuclear arsenal and command-and-control system capable of absorbing a nuclear strike and launching a retaliatory strike that would inflict unacceptable damage on the adversary. See *assured destruction capability.*

MX missile: A MIRVed, fixed, land-based ballistic missile with ten warheads; the United States intends to deploy fifty MXs in Minuteman silos.

maneuvering reentry vehicle (MARV): A reentry vehicle carried by a ballistic missile and capable of altering course during flight (making it more difficult for ABM systems to intercept and destroy).

massive retaliation: A strategy that prepared for large-scale nuclear attack in response to aggression by the adversary; formally adopted as NATO doctrine in 1956.

medium-range ballistic missile (MRBM): A ballistic missile with a range of approximately 500 to 1500 miles. See *ballistic missile.*

Midgetman missile: A single-warhead, mobile, land-based ballistic missile under development by the United States.

Minuteman missile: The major U.S. intercontinental ballistic missile (ICBM); 450 single-warhead Minuteman II and 550 three-warhead Minuteman III missiles are currently deployed (50 Minuteman III missiles are scheduled to be replaced by MX missiles).

multiple independently targetable reentry vehicle (MIRV): One of two or more reentry vehicles carried by one ballistic missile but capable of being directed to individual targets.

nuclear parity: A balance of nuclear forces such that each side is deterred from initiating their use.

nuclear threshold: The point at which nuclear weapons are first used by either side (i.e., efforts to reduce reliance on nuclear weapons are attempts to "raise the nuclear threshold").

nuclear warhead: Explosive component of a nuclear weapon.

nuclear weapon: Refers to a nuclear warhead coupled with its delivery system; includes short-range ("tactical" or "battlefield"), medium-range, intermediate-range, and long-range ("strategic") weapons.

Pershing II missile: Highly accurate medium-range ballistic missile deployed in Western Europe.

preemptive strike: A strike launched in anticipation of an opponent's nuclear strike.

reentry vehicle (RV): The portion of a ballistic missile that carries the nuclear warhead through its trajectory in outer space and during its reentry into the atmosphere.

sea-launched ballistic missile (SLBM): A ballistic missile launched from a submarine. See *ballistic missile.*

submarine-launched ballistic missile: See *sea-launched ballistic missile.*

Second Strategic Arms Limitation Talks (SALT II) Treaty: An arms control agreement signed by the United States and the Soviet Union in 1979 but unratified by the U.S. Senate; sets ceilings on U.S. and Soviet strategic forces. Until June 1986, when the U.S. repudiated the agreement, each side had pledged to "not undercut" its provisions.

second strike: A retaliatory nuclear attack in response to a strategic nuclear strike by the adversary.

second use: The responsive use of nuclear weapons by one side following first use of such weapons by the other side. (Compare *follow-on use.*)

Star Wars: The popular name for the U.S. Strategic Defense Initiative, a research, development, and testing program to create the means to intercept strategic ballistic missiles in all phases of flight.

Star Wars I: President Reagan's vision of an impenetrable shield to defend the nation's population against nuclear attack; the defensive shield would be substituted for offensive nuclear forces.

Star Wars II: The vision of SDI supported by most U.S. officials and outside proponents; foresees imperfect defenses for a variety of purposes, such as defense of military assets or partial protection of the population; the defenses would supplement the offensive nuclear forces.

Strategic Defense Initiative (SDI): See *Star Wars.*

strategic nuclear weapon: Weapon based in the United States, the Soviet Union, or at sea, capable of striking targets in the adversary's homeland. (See *nuclear weapon.*)

sustained engagement: The policy of establishing and maintaining long-term political, economic, and cultural ties between the East and West.

tactical nuclear weapon: A short-range weapon intended for the limited purpose of affecting a specific military situation. (See *nuclear weapon.*)

theater nuclear forces: Nuclear forces based in a region in which they would be used; includes short-, medium-, and intermediate-range nuclear forces; usually applied to weapons based in Europe.

time-urgent target: A target that can be more easily located or destroyed early in a conflict; includes bombers still on the ground and nuclear munitions still concentrated in storage sites.

Notes

1. THE RISK OF WAR

5 *Einstein:* Letter of August 2, 1939 reprinted in Otto Nathan and Heinz Norden, eds., *Einstein on Peace* (New York: Simon & Schuster, 1960), pp. 294–96.

5 *Rogers:* "Tough Talk from NATO's General Rogers," *Business Week,* July 22, 1985, p. 122D; Robert Hutchinson, "NATO Ministers Can't Abdicate CW Decision, Says SACEUR," *Jane's Defence Weekly,* April 27, 1985, p. 719.

14 *Tuchman:* Barbara W. Tuchman, *The Guns of August* (New York: Bantam, 1962), p. 91.

2. THE FIRST HALF CENTURY OF THE NUCLEAR AGE

19 *Evolution:* An excellent brief history of NATO's conception of the role of nuclear weapons is presented in J. Michael Legge, "Theater Nuclear Weapons and the NATO Strategy of Flexible Response," Santa Monica, Calif.: Rand Corporation, publication R2964-FF, April 1983. For this section I have also drawn on David N. Schwartz, "A Historical Perspective," in John Steinbruner and Leon Sigal, eds., *Alliance Security: NATO and the No-First-Use Question* (Washington, D.C.: Brookings Institution, 1983), pp. 5–21.

20 *defense guidance:* George C. Wilson, "Preparing for Long Nuclear War Is Waste of Funds, General Jones Says," *Washington Post,* June 19, 1982.

21 *Dulles:* John Foster Dulles, "The Evolution of Foreign Policy,"

Department of State Bulletin 30, no. 761 (January 25, 1954), p. 108.

22 *Montgomery:* Address to the Royal United Services Institute, London, cited in Robert E. Osgood, *NATO: The Entangling Alliance,* (Chicago: University of Chicago Press, 1962), p. 110.

25 *a matter of hours:* "Tough Talk from NATO's General Rogers," *Business Week,* July 22, 1985, p. 122D; Robert Hutchinson, "NATO Ministers Can't Abdicate CW Decision, Says SACEUR," *Jane's Defence Weekly,* April 27, 1985, p. 719.

25 *American public:* Public Agenda Foundation, *Voter Options on Nuclear Arms Policy: A Briefing Book for the 1984 Elections* (New York: Public Agenda Foundation, 1984), p. 34.

26 *Soviet Nuclear Strategy:* Much of the following discussion is based on James M. McConnell, "The Shift in Soviet Military Development from Nuclear to Conventional." Unpublished manuscript.

27 *opponents of nuclear arms control:* See, for example, Richard H. Pipes, "Why the Soviet Union Thinks It Could Fight and Win a Nuclear War," *Commentary,* July 1977, p. 21.

27 *Brezhnev:* U.S. Arms Control and Disarmament Agency, *Documents on Disarmament, 1982* (Washington, D.C.: GPO, 1986), p. 350.

27 *Ustinov:* D. F. Ustinov, "We Serve the Homeland and the Cause of Communism," *Izvestia,* May 27, 1982.

28 *An Evaluation of Plans for the Use of Nuclear Weapons:* For this section I have drawn on Arms Control Association, *Arms Control and National Security,* (Washington, D.C.: Arms Control Association, 1983); and William Kaufmann, "Nuclear Deterrence in Central Europe," and Leon V. Sigal, "No First Use and NATO's Nuclear Posture," in Steinbruner and Sigal, *Alliance Security.*

29 *Kissinger:* Henry A. Kissinger, "NATO Defense and the Soviet Threat," *Survival,* November/December 1979, p. 266 (address in Brussels).

30 *NATO nuclear weapons:* Arms Control Association, *Arms Control and National Security;* William A. Arkin, Thomas B. Cochran, and Milton M. Hoenig, "Resource Paper on the U.S. Nuclear Arsenal," *Bulletin of the Atomic Scientists,* August/September 1984, p. 10s.

32 *Current guidelines: NATO Facts and Figures,* 10th ed. (Brussels: NATO Information Service, 1981), pp. 152–54.

32 *follow-on use of nuclear weapons:* North Atlantic Assembly's Special Committee on Nuclear Weapons in Europe, *Second Interim Report on Nuclear Weapons in Europe,* report to the U.S. Senate Committee on Foreign Relations, 98th Cong., sess. (Washington, D.C.: GPO, 1983), p. 7.

32 *nuclear explosions:* A 100-kiloton tactical nuclear weapon would be needed to destroy approximately fifty to one hundred armored fighting vehicles (e.g., tanks) in dispersed formation, the equivalent of a regiment. Such a weapon would create general destruction (of structures and people) in a circle with a diameter of 4.5 miles (an area of 15 square miles). A blast circle of this size, in typical Western European countries, would be likely to include two or three villages or towns of several thousand persons. In addition, depending on the nature of the weapon and the height of the burst, a much larger area could be affected by fallout. Several hundred of such tactical nuclear weapons would be required to counter an armored development in Europe. See Seymour J. Deitchman, *New Technology and Military Power* (Boulder, Colo.: Westview Press, 1979), p. 12.

33 *Schmidt:* Helmut Schmidt, *Defense or Retaliation?* (New York: Praeger, 1962), p. 101. Schmidt's comment and the exercise result are cited in Jeffrey Record, *U.S. Nuclear Weapons in Europe,* (Washington, D.C.: Brookings Institution, 1974), pp.10–11.

33 *former aides:* Alain C. Enthoven and K. Wayne Smith, *How Much is Enough?* (New York: Harper & Row, 1971), p. 128.

34 *group of experts: General and Complete Disarmament: A Comprehensive Study on Nuclear Weapons: Report of the Secretary General, Fall 1980* (New York: United Nations, 1981), passim.

35 *chaos on the battlefield:* This discussion is based on a presentation by Vice Admiral John M. Lee (ret.) in St. Petersburg, Florida, December 17, 1981.

35 *retired Chiefs of the British Defense Staffs:* Solly Zuckerman, *Nuclear Illusion and Reality* (New York: Viking, 1982), pp. 70–71.

3. NUCLEAR MYTHS

40 *win the arms race:* See, for example, Public Agenda Foundation, *Voter Options On Nuclear Arms Policy: A Briefing Book for the 1984 Elections* (New York: Public Agenda Foundation, 1984), p. 24; L. H. Gelb, "Poll Finds Doubt on U.S. Strategy on the Russians," *New York Times,* April 15, 1983.

40 *Kirkpatrick:* Jeane Kirkpatrick, "The Russian Advantage," *Washington Post,* January 5, 1986.

40 *Reagan's views:* President's news conference, September 17, 1985, in *Weekly Compilation of Presidential Documents* (Washington, D.C.: GPO, 1985), p. 1106.

40 *Nitze:* Paul H. Nitze, "Is SALT II a Fair Deal for the United States?" (May 16, 1979), reprinted in Charles Tyroler II, ed., *Alerting America: The Papers of the Committee on the Present Danger* (Washington, D.C.: Pergamon-Brassey's International Defense Publishers, 1985), p. 160.

41 *Nunn's response:* Sam Nunn, "How to Make the Summit Productive," *Washington Post,* October 2, 1985.

41 *Table 3:* For sources see Appendix III.

42 *Weinberger:* Secretary of Defense Caspar Weinberger, "Strategic Defense and American Strategy," speech to the Philadelphia World Affairs Council, October 3, 1985. Mimeographed.

42 *Gershwin:* Testimony of June 26, 1985, by Lawrence K. Gersh-

win, national intelligence officer for strategic programs, Central Intelligence Agency, before the Subcommittee on Strategic and Theater Nuclear Forces of the Committee on Armed Services and the Subcommittee on Defense of the Committee on Appropriations, in U.S. Congress, Senate, Committee on Armed Forces and Committee on Appropriations, *Soviet Strategic Force Developments* (Washington, D.C.: GPO, 1985), p. 17.

42 *Jones:* Leon V. Sigal, "Warming to the Freeze," *Foreign Policy* 48 (Fall 1982): p. 61.

43 *Vessey:* Testimony of May 11, 1982, in U.S. Congress, Senate, Committee on Armed Services, *Nomination of General John Vessey to be Chairman, Joint Chiefs of Staff,* cited in *New York Times,* May 12, 1982.

43 *Crowe:* Testimony before the Senate Committee on Armed Services, February 5, 1986. In a written response to questions from the committee, the Joint Chiefs of Staff stated, "None of us would trade our overall strategic nuclear forces with the Soviets." See U.S. Congress, Senate Committee on Armed Services, *MX Missile Basing System and Related Issues* (Washington, D.C.: GPO, 1983), p. 226.

43 *Scowcroft:* "Report of the President's Commission on Strategic Forces," April 1983, pp. 7–8. Mimeographed.

46 *Alsop:* Stewart Alsop, "Our New Strategy: The Alternatives to Total War," *Saturday Evening Post,* December 1, 1962, pp. 13–18.

47 *Committee on the Present Danger:* "What Is the Soviet Union Up To?" (April 4, 1977), cited in Robert Scheer, *With Enough Shovels: Reagan, Bush and Nuclear War* (New York: Random House, 1982), pp. 51, 37–38.

48 *SS-25:* Memorandum for the President on "Responding to Soviet Violations Policy (RSVP) Study," November 13, 1985, p. 10.

48 *Reagan:* Question-and-answer session with newspaper editors, October 16, 1981, in *Weekly Compilation,* p. 957.

48 *Soviet ICBMs:* For discussion see two articles by Paul Nitze: "Deterring Our Deterrent," *Foreign Policy,* no. 25 (Winter 1976–77): 195–210; "Assuring Strategic Stability in an Era of Detente," *Foreign Affairs,* January 1976, pp. 207–32.

49 *Scowcroft commission:* "Report of the President's Commission on Strategic Forces," pp. 7–8.

50 *Thunman:* "Navy Says No Foreseeable Threat to Submarines," *Defense Daily,* March 15, 1985, p. 85.

50 *Brezhnev:* Cited in Raymond L. Garthoff, *Détente and Confrontation* (Washington, D.C.: Brookings Institution, 1985), p. 769.

50 *"not for deterrence":* Dusko Doder, "Soviets Blast Reagan Plan to Build MX," (*Washington Post,* October 4, 1981), cited in Scheer, *With Enough Shovels,* p. 78.

50 *Andropov:* Yuri Andropov, interview with *Pravda,* March 27, 1983, press release from Soviet embassy, Washington, D.C.

51 *Air Force document:* Memorandum from Secretary of Defense Robert S. McNamara to President John F. Kennedy, "Recommended FY1964–FY1968 Strategic Retaliatory Forces," November 21, 1962, p. 6.

52 *Reagan:* Address to the nation, November 22, 1982, in *Weekly Compilation,* p. 1508.

59 *Star Wars speech:* Address to the nation, March 23, 1983, in *Weekly Compilation,* p. 443.

59 *Keyworth:* George A. Keyworth, "The Case for Strategic Defense: An Option for a World Disarmed," *Issues in Science and Technology,* Fall 1984, p. 44; R. Jeffrey Smith, "The Search for a Nuclear Sanctuary," *Science* 221 (July 1, 1983): 32.

60 *Wagner:* Testimony of March 18, 1983, U.S. Congress, House, Armed Services Committee, *Department of Energy National Security and Military Applications of Nuclear Energy Act of 1984,* (Washington, D.C.: GPO, 1983), pp. 28, 33.

61 *Table 5:* For source see Appendix II.

62 *Harriman:* Foreword by W. Averell Harrimann to Edward M.

Kennedy and Mark O. Hatfield, *Freeze!* (New York: Bantam, 1982), p. iv.

64 *Limited Test Ban:* For a fuller discussion see Glenn T. Seaborg, *Kennedy, Khrushchev, and the Test Ban* (Berkeley: University of California Press, 1981).

64 *293 nuclear tests:* Ibid., p. 288.

66 *Smith:* Gerard Smith, *Doubletalk: The Story of SALT I* (Garden City, N.Y.: Doubleday, 1980), p. 169.

66 *Kissinger:* Press briefing, December 1974, quoted ibid., p. 177.

67 *Perle:* Fred Hiatt, "Perle's Distrust Shapes U.S. Policy," *Washington Post,* January 2, 1985.

68 *ABM Treaty:* For discussion see "The President's Unclassified Report of Noncompliance with Arms Control Agreements," December 23, 1985; Arms Control Association, *Countdown on SALT II,* (Washington, D.C.: Arms Control Association, 1985; Thomas K. Longstreth, John E. Pike, and John B. Rhinelander, "The Impact of U.S. and Soviet Ballistic Missile Defense Programs on the ABM Treaty," report for the National Campaign to Save the ABM Treaty, March 1985.

68 *Warnke:* Interview with Robert Scheer, Spring 1981, cited in Scheer, *With Enough Shovels,* p. 38.

68 *Chain:* Testimony of February 20, 1985, in U.S. Congress, Senate, Committee on Armed Services, *Soviet Treaty Violations,* (Washington, D.C.: GPO, 1985) p. 44. Current U.S. commissioner to the SCC, Ambassador Richard H. Ellis, is reported to have credited the Soviets with general SALT compliance in secret testimony to the House Intelligence Committee on November 20, 1985; see Rowland Evans and Robert Novak, "SALT Sabotage," *Washington Post,* December 18, 1985.

69 *submarines dismantled:* Arms Control Association, *Countdown on Salt II,* p. 2.

69 *Weinberger:* Testimony of April 21, 1983, in U.S. Congress, House, Committee on Armed Services, *Department of Defense*

Authorization of Appropriations for Fiscal Year 1984 (Washington, D.C.: GPO, 1983), p. 156.

70 *joint paper:* U.S. Departments of State and Defense and Arms Control and Disarmament Agency, background paper in response to the film *The SALT Syndrome,* June 1980.

70 *the Pentagon:* RSVP study, p. 9.

70 *SCC process:* For discussion see Walter Pincus, "Agencies Split on Response to Possible ABM Treaty Violtions," *Washington Post,* December 19, 1985; Sidney N. Graybeal and Michael Krepon, "Making Better Use of the Standing Consultative Commission," *International Security* 10, no. 2 (Fall 1985): 183–99.

71 *deployment of the Midgetman:* "Reagan Statement on Arms Accord," *New York Times,* June 11, 1985.

71 *Scowcroft commission:* "President's Commission on Strategic Forces, Second Report," March 21, 1984, p. 7. Mimeographed.

72 *Weinberger:* Caspar Weinberger, presentation before the House Budget Committee, March 20, 1981, cited in Scheer, *With Enough Shovels,* pp. 162–63.

72 *Perle:* Hiatt, "Perle's Distrust Shapes U.S. Policy,"

72 *Reagan:* Debate with President Carter, October 28, 1980, *Public Papers of the Presidents: Administration of Jimmy Carter, 1980,* (Washington, D. C.: GPO, 1981), p. 2489.

4. THE NEXT HALF CENTURY

79 *nuclear-weapons-building program:* Walter Pincus, "Funds Sought for Expansion of Nuclear Arms Production," *Washington Post,* April 8, 1986.

80 *Los Alamos:* William J. Broad, "U.S. Researchers Foresee Big Rise in Nuclear Tests," *New York Times,* April 21, 1986.

81 *panel's report:* Aspen Institute International Group, *Managing East-West Conflict: A Framework for Sustained Engagement* (New York: Aspen Institute for Humanistic Studies, 1984).

85 *Kennan:* Address by George F. Kennan, "A Proposal for International Disarmament," Washington, D.C., May 19, 1981 (reprinted by the Institute for World Order).

86 *Gorbachev:* Soviet embassy, Washington, D.C., "Statement by Mikhail Gorbachev," news release, January 16, 1986.

86 *"general and complete disarmament":* See, for example, "Soviet Statement Submitted During the Bilateral Talks with the United States, June 27, 1961," pp. 199–213; and "United States Declaration Submitted to the General Assembly: A Program for General and Complete Disarmament in a Peaceful World, September 25, 1961," pp. 475–82—both in U.S. Arms Control and Disarmament Agency, *Documents on Disarmament, 1961* (Washington, D.C.: GPO, 1962).

86 *Reagan:* Inaugural address, January 20, 1985, in *Weekly Compilation of Presidential Documents* (Washington, D.C.: GPO, 1985), p. 69.

86 *Carter:* Inaugural address, January 20, 1977, in *Weekly Compilation,* p. 3.

87 *Brzezinski:* John J. Fialka and Frederick Kempe, "U.S. Welcomes Soviet Arms Plan, but Dismisses Part as Propaganda," *Wall Street Journal,* January 17, 1986.

89 *March 23 speech:* Address to the nation, March 23, 1983, in *Weekly Compilation,* pp. 447–48.

90 *March 29:* Address to the National Space Club, March 29, 1985, in *Weekly Compilation,* p. 380.

91 *August 22:* Remarks at a California Republican Party fundraising dinner, Los Angeles, August 22, 1985, in *Weekly Compilation,* p. 996.

91 *joint session:* Address of November 21, 1985, in *Weekly Compilation,* p. 1427.

91 *Abrahamson:* R. Jeffrey Smith, "Star Wars Chief Takes Aim at Critics," *Science,* August 10, 1984, p. 600; testimony of May 9, 1984, in U.S. Congress, House, Committee on Appropriations, *Department of Defense Authorization for Appropriations for Fiscal Year 1986* (Washington, D.C.: GPO, 1985), p. 732.

93 *Teller:* Quoted in Richard L. Garwin, "Space Defense—the Impossible Dream," *NATO's Sixteen Nations*, April 1986, pp. 22–23.

94 *Iklé:* Testimony of February 21, 1985, in U.S. Congress, Senate, Committee on Armed Services, *Department of Defense Authorization for Appropriations for Fiscal Year 1986* (Washington, D.C.: GPO, 1985), p. 3515.

94 *Toomay:* John C. Toomay, "The Case for Ballistic Missile Defense," *Daedalus*, Summer 1985, p. 233.

94 *Cooper:* Testimony of March 8, 1984, in U.S. Congress, Senate, Committee on Armed Services, *Department of Defense Authorization for Appropriations for Fiscal Year 1985* (Washington, D.C.: GPO, 1984), p. 2925.

94 *De Lauer:* Testimony of November 10, 1983, in U.S. Congress, House, Committee on Armed Services, *Hearings on H.R. 3073: People Protection Act* (Washington, D.C.: GPO, 1984), pp. 21–22, 26.

94 *space-based laser defense:* Introduced into the record by Senator Larry Pressler at April 25, 1984, hearing. U.S. Congress, Senate, Committee on Foreign Relations, *Strategic Defense and Anti-Satellite Weapons* (Washington, D.C.: GPO, 1984), p. 67.

95 *$1 trillion:* James R. Schlesinger, banquet address, in *National Security Issues Symposium 1984: Space, National Security, and C31; October 25 and 26, 1984,* MITRE document M85-3, pp. 56, 61; Harold Brown, "The Strategic Defense Initiative: Defensive Systems and the Strategic Debate," paper released by the Foreign Policy Institute, School of Advanced International Studies, Johns Hopkins University, December 14, 1984, p. 14. Brown's estimate includes the cost of air defense and civil defense. Schlesinger's is for antiballistic missile systems only.

95 *annual expenditure:* Harold Brown, testimony before the Senate Appropriations Committee, April 10, 1986, preliminary stenographic transcript from Senate committee; cited in Rich-

ard L. Garwin and John Pike, "History and Current Debate," *Bulletin of the Atomic Scientists,* May 1984, p. 45.

95 *Reagan's claims:* Weekly radio address to the nation, October 12, 1985, White House mimeograph; remarks to the American Legion, September 4, 1984, in *Weekly Compilation,* p. 1223.

95 *Schlesinger:* James R. Schlesinger, banquet address, in *National Security Issues Symposium 1984: Space, National Security, and C31: October 25 and 26, 1984,* MITRE document M85-3, p. 57.

95 *Brown:* Harold Brown, "The Strategic Defense Initiative," pp. 3, 6.

96 *Kissinger:* Henry A. Kissinger, "Should We Try to Defend Against Russia's Missiles?" *Washington Post,* September 23, 1984.

96 *Brzezinski and Max Kampelman:* Zbigniew Brzezinski, Robert Jastrow, Max M. Kampelman, "Defense in Space Is Not 'Star Wars,' " *New York Times Magazine,* January 27, 1985.

96 *Abrahamson:* Testimony of March 19, 1985, in U.S. Congress, House, Committee on Armed Services, *Hearings on H.R. 1872* (Washington, D.C.: GPO, 1985), p. 351.

97 *White House: The President's Strategic Defense Initiative,* White House paper, January 1985, p. 3.

97 *Hoffman:* Testimony of March 1, 1985, in U.S. Congress, Senate, Committee on Armed Services, *Department of Defense Authorization for Appropriations for Fiscal Year 1986* (Washington, D.C.: GPO, 1985), p. 3629.

97 *Directive 172:* U.S. Department of State, *The Strategic Defense Initiative,* Special Report no. 129, June 1985, p. 307. According to press reports, this document is a declassified version of National Security Decision Directive 172, May 30, 1985.

97 *Nitze:* Paul H. Nitze, "U.S. Strategic Force Structures: The Challenge Ahead," address to the American Institute of Aeronautics and Astronautics Strategic Systems Conference, Monterey, California, February 4, 1986, U.S. Department of State, Current Policy no. 794, p. 1.

98 *"no one wants that"*: Address to the nation, March 23, 1983, in *Weekly Compilation*, p. 448.

98 *"most dangerous thing"*: Interview with representatives of the *Baltimore Sun*, March 12, 1986, in *Weekly Compilation*, p. 347.

99 *"In 1946"*: Remarks at a question-and-answer session at a Los Angeles World Affairs Council luncheon, March 31, 1983, in *Weekly Compilation*, p. 480.

99 *"know perfectly well"*: Remarks on NBC television's "Meet the Press," March 27, 1983, NBC transcript, p. 10.

99 *"I can assure you"*: Interview with Soviet journalists, the White House, October 31, 1985, in *Weekly Compilation*, p. 1349.

99 *LeMay:* "Document One: Memorandum OP-36c/jm, 18 March 1954," appendix to David Alan Rosenberg, "A Smoking, Radiating Ruin at the End of Two Hours," *International Security*, Winter 1981, p. 27.

99 *Air Force proposals:* Memorandum from Secretary of Defense Robert S. McNamara to President Kennedy, "Recommended FY1964–FY1968 Strategic Retaliatory Forces, November 21, 1962, p. 6."

99 *Secretary Weinberger says:* Testimony of January 6, 1981, in U.S. Congress, Senate, Committee on Armed Services, *Nomination of Caspar W. Weinberger to be Secretary of Defense* (Washington, D.C.: GPO, 1981), p. 20.

100 *"retaliatory strike capacity"*: Question-and-answer session with reporters, the White House, October 16, 1981, in *Weekly Compilation*, p. 957.

100 *Perle:* Testimony of May 7, 1985, in U.S. Congress, Senate, Committee on Armed Services, *Soviet Treaty Violations* (Washington, D.C.: GPO, 1985), p. 9

100 *"a more destabilizing factor"*: Gerald F. Seib, "Officials Say Reagan Is Ready to Spend Billions Researching Lasers, Weapons of 21st-Century War," *Wall Street Journal*, December 7, 1983.

101 *"a monopoly position"*: "Maintaining Defense Despite Soviet

Disinformation," interview published in the *Washington Times*, May 13, 1985.

101 *"seeking a first-strike capability":* Caspar W. Weinberger, "Morality Demands the SDI As Only Alternative to US-Soviet Suicide Pact," *New York City Tribune*, January 2, 1986.

101 *threats to use nuclear weapons:* Truman: *Public Papers of the Presidents: Harry S. Truman, 1950* (Washington, D.C.: GPO, 1965), p. 727; Eisenhower: Dwight D. Eisenhower, *Mandate for Change, 1953–56* (New York: Signet, 1963), p. 230; Nixon: Richard Nixon, *RN* (New York: Grosset & Dunlap, 1978), pp. 393–414, and H. R. Haldeman, *The Ends of Power* (New York: Times Books, 1978), pp. 82–83; Carter: Jimmy Carter, *Keeping Faith: Memoirs of a President* (New York: Bantam, 1982), p. 483.

101 *benefits of SDI technology:* See the remarks of Secretary of Defense Weinberger at the German-American Roundtable, Bonn, West Germany, December 5, 1985, excerpted in U.S. Department of Defense, *Selected Statements*, December 1985, p. 6; Abrahamson testimony of May 7, 1985, in U.S. Congress, House, Committee on Appropriations, *Department of Defense Appropriations for Fiscal Year 1986* (Washington, D.C.: GPO, 1985), p. 640.

102 *"more effective defense":* Quoted in Charles Mohr, "Star Wars in Strategy: The Russian Response," *New York Times*, December 17, 1985.

102 *"a system which is effective":* Testimony of February 1, 1984, in U.S. Congress, Senate, Committee on Armed Services, *Department of Defense Authorization for Appropriations for Fiscal Year 1986* (Washington, D.C.: GPO, 1984), p. 89.

102 *"a fairy tale":* Nationally televised address, June 26, 1985, quoted in Office of Technology Assessment, *Ballistic Missile Defense Technologies* (Washington, D.C.: GPO, 1985), p. 314.

102 *"share their experience":* Geneva press conference of November 21, 1985. Soviet embassy, Washington, D.C., "Mikhail

Gorbachev's Press Conference," November 26, 1985, p. 8. Mimeographed.

103 *"plans could be executed"*: Memorandum for the President on "Responding to Soviet Violations Policy (RSVP) Study," November 13, 1985, quoted in Walter Pincus, "Weinberger Urges Buildup over Soviet 'Violations,'" *Washington Post,* November 18, 1985.

103 *"We are aware of that"*: Testimony of February 4, 1985, in U.S. Congress, Senate, Committee on Armed Services, *Department of Defense Authorization for Appropriations for Fiscal Year 1986* (Washington, D.C.: GPO, 1985), p. 91.

104 *Brown:* Brown, "Is SDI Technically Feasible?" *Foreign Affairs, America and the World 1985,* p. 450.

104 *Defensive Technologies Study Team:* Summary statement, quoted in written statement of James C. Fletcher, chairman, submitted to the Senate Armed Services Committee, March 8, 1984, in U.S. Congress, Senate, Committee on Armed Services, *Department of Defense Authorization for Appropriations for Fiscal Year 1985* (Washington, D.C.: GPO, 1984), p. 2919.

104 *"strategic concept"*: Nitze, "SDI: Its Nature and Rationale," U.S. Department of State, Current Policy no. 751, p. 3.

105 *Schlesinger:* Schlesinger, "The Eagle and the Bear," *Foreign Affairs,* Summer 1985, p. 960.

105 *"tricky"*: Nitze, "On the Road to a More Stable Peace," address to the Philadelphia World Affairs Council, February 20, 1985, p. 7. Mimeographed.

105 *Office of Technology Assessment:* U.S. Congress, Office of Technology Assessment, *Ballistic Missile Defense Technologies* (Washington, D.C.: GPO, 1985), pp. 13, 11.

107 *Nitze:* Nitze, "U.S. Strategic Force Structures," p. 2.

107 *Reagan:* Interview with representatives of the wire services, November 6, 1985, in *Weekly Compilation,* p. 1359. Reagan had told Soviet journalists on October 31, "We won't put this weapon—or this system in place, this defensive system, until

we do away with our nuclear missiles, our offensive missiles,"
(*Weekly Compilation*, p. 1343). White House spokesman
Larry Speakes labeled that remark "presidential imprecision";
Lou Cannon, "Reagan Remark on SDI Called an 'Impreci-
sion,'" *Washington Post*, November 6, 1985.

108 *report to the Congress: Annual Report to the Congress, Fiscal
Year 1987*, February 5, 1986, p. 292.

108 *Abrahamson:* Written response to question in conjunction
with testimony of February 27, 1985, in U.S. Congress, House,
Committee on Armed Services, *The MX Missile and the Strategic Defense Initiative—Their Implications on Arms Control
Negotiations* (Washington, D.C.: GPO, 1985), p. 34.

109 *"should be assessed collectively":* "Report of the President's
Commission on Strategic Forces," April 1983, p. 8. Mimeographed.

110 *Smith:* Gerard Smith, "Star Wars Is Still the Problem," *Arms
Control Today*, March 1986, p. 6.

110 *Keyworth:* George A. Keyworth, "The Case for Strategic Defense: An Option for a World Disarmed," *Issues in Science and
Technology*, Fall 1984, p. 44.

112 *Carver: Sunday Times* (London), February 21, 1982.

112 *Gayler: Congressional Record*, 97th Cong., 1st sess., July 17,
1981 (Washington, D.C.: GPO, 1981), p. S7835.

112 *Steinhoff:* Hans Gunther Brauch "The Enhanced Radiation
Warhead: A West German Perspective," *Arms Control Today*,
June 1978, p. 3.

112 *Kissinger:* Kissinger, "NATO Defense and the Soviet Threat,"
Survival, November/December 1979, p. 266.

113 *Laird:* Melvin R. Laird, "What Our Defense Really Needs,"
Washington Post, April 12, 1982.

113 *"I pray":* Reagan remarks at ceremony for presidential scholar
awards, June 16, 1983, *Weekly Compilation*, p. 875.

113 *"Our goal":* Address to the nation, February 26, 1986, in
Weekly Compilation, p. 289.

119 *Rogers:* General Bernard W. Rogers, "The Atlantic Alliance:

Prescripts for a Difficult Decade," *Foreign Affairs,* Summer 1982, pp. 1145–46.

119 *Kaufmann:* William W. Kaufmann, "Nonnuclear Deterrence," in John D. Steinbruner and Leon V. Sigal, eds., *Alliance Security: NATO and the No-First-Use Question* (Washington, D.C.: Brookings Institution, 1983), pp. 43–90.

119 *international study group:* European Security Study, *Strengthening Conventional Deterrence in Europe* (New York: St. Martin's, 1983).

120 *Nunn: Congressional Record,* 98th Cong., 1st sess., July 13, 1983, (Washington, D.C.: GPO, 1983), p. 9853.

123 *"adequacy for deterrence alone":* David Alan Rosenberg, "The Origins of Overkill: Nuclear Weapons and American Strategy, 1945–1960," *International Security,* Spring 1983, pp. 56–57.

124 *Tactical nuclear weapons:* The withdrawal of one thousand tactical nuclear warheads agreed to in the December 1979 NATO communiqué has been completed. At a 1983 meeting in Montebello, Canada, NATO members agreed to further net reductions of fourteen hundred nuclear warheads from Europe. After these adjustments roughly forty-five hundred nuclear warheads will remain in Europe.

5. GENEVA: A STEP TOWARD OUR LONG-TERM GOAL

127 *Nitze:* Paul H. Nitze, "On the Road to a More Stable Peace," address to the Philadelphia World Affairs Council, February 20, 1985, p. 7. Mimeographed.

129 *"reasonably confident decision":* Testimony of March 15, 1985, in U.S. Congress, Senate, Committee on Armed Services, *Department of Defense Authorization for Appropriations for Fiscal Year 1986* (Washington, D.C.: GPO, 1985), p. 3985.

129 *"It's going to go up":* Pat Jefferson, " 'Can Do' Abrahamson:

Weave ABM Technology into Arms Control Strategy," *Aerospace America,* July 1984, p. 20.

6. TURNING AWAY FROM NUCLEAR DISASTER

136 *"Dig a hole"*: Thomas K. Jones, deputy under secretary of defense for research and engineering, strategic and theater nuclear forces, quoted in Robert Scheer, *With Enough Shovels: Reagan, Bush and Nuclear War* (New York: Random House, 1982), pp. 18, 21, 25.

137 *"Japan, after all"*: From the confirmation hearings of Eugene V. Rostow to be director of the United States Arms Control and Disarmament Agency, June 22, 1981, in U.S. Congress, Senate, Committee on Foreign Relations, *Nomination of Eugene V. Rostow* (Washington, D.C.: GPO, 1981), pp. 48–49.

137 *"I think it is possible"*: Charles Kupperman, executive director, General Advisory Committee on Arms Control and Disarmament, interview with Robert Scheer, Fall 1981, in Scheer, *With Enough Shovels,* pp. 184–85.

137 *Bush:* George Bush, candidate for the Republican presidential nomination, interview with Robert Scheer of the *Los Angeles Times,* January 1980, from Scheer, *With Enough Shovels,* p. 29.

137 *Bundy:* McGeorge Bundy, "To Cap the Volcano," *Foreign Affairs,* October 1969, p. 2.

138 *health problems:* Jay Mathews, "Chernobyl May Affect 100,000: Dr. Gale Discusses Plan to Monitor Residents' Health," *Washington Post,* May 19, 1986.

139 *Mendelsohn:* Boyce Rensberger, "Chernobyl and Shuttle: Lessons for East and West," *International Herald Tribune,* May 7, 1986.

APPENDIX V. THE STAR WARS DEFENSE SYSTEM

Abrahamson, Lieutenant General James. News briefing at the Pentagon, November 26, 1985. Department of Defense. Photocopy.

————. Statement on the Strategic Defense Initiative. Testimony before the House Armed Services Committee, March 4, 1986. Photocopy.

Bethe, Hans A., Jeffrey Boutwell, and Richard L. Garwin. "BMD Technologies and Concepts in the 1980s." *Daedalus*, Spring 1985, pp. 53–71.

————, Richard L. Garwin, Kurt Gottfried, and Henry W. Kendall. "Space-based Ballistic-Missile Defense." *Scientific American*, October 1984, pp. 39–49.

Brown, Harold. "Is SDI Technically Feasible?" *Foreign Affairs*, America and the World 1985, pp. 435–54.

Defensive Technologies Study Team (Fletcher panel). "The Strategic Defense Initiative: Defensive Technologies Study," summary, March 1984. In U.S. Congress. Senate. Committee on Foreign Relations. *Strategic Defense and Anti-Satellite Weapons*, pp. 141–75. Washington, D.C.: GPO, 1984.

Drell, Sidney D., and Wolfgang K. H. Panofsky. "The Case Against Strategic Defense: Technical and Strategic Realities." *Issues in Science and Technology*, Fall 1984, pp. 45–65.

Pike, John. "The Emperor's Newest Clothing: Changes to the SDI as a Result of Phase-I Architecture Studies," February 16, 1986. Unpublished paper.

Scheer, Robert. "Flaws Peril Pivotal 'Star Wars' Laser." *Los Angeles Times*, September 23, 1985.

Smith, R. Jeffrey. "Experts Cast Doubts on X-Ray Laser." *Science*, November 8, 1985, pp. 646–48.

U.S. Congress. House. Committee on Appropriations. *Department of Defense Appropriations for 1984.* Washington, D.C.: GPO, 1983.

U.S. Congress. Office of Technology Assessment, *Ballistic Missile Defense Technologies.* Washington, D.C.: GPO, 1985.

U.S. Department of Defense. *Report to Congress on the Strategic Defense Initiative 1986,* May 1986 draft.

Waller, Douglas, James Bruce, and Douglas Cook. "SDI: Progress and Challenges." Staff report submitted to Senators William Proxmire, J. Bennett Johnston, and Lawton Chiles, March 17, 1986.

Yonas, Gerold. "Strategic Defense Initiative: The Politics and Science of Weapons in Space." *Physics Today,* June 1985.

Acknowledgments

I n December 1960, when President-elect Kennedy asked me to serve in his cabinet as Secretary of Defense, I had taught at the Harvard Graduate School of Business Administration as an assistant professor; served in the U.S. Army in World War II as a lieutenant colonel; and, a short time before, been elected president of Ford Motor Company. It was hardly a background that qualified me for the position Kennedy offered. After I pointed this out, he remarked he wasn't aware of any school for Presidents either. So I accepted. But it was with the clear understanding—an agreement from which he never once deviated—that I would staff the upper echelons of the department with the brightest people I could find, without regard to partisan political considerations.

That is how there came to be assembled the ablest group of individuals to serve together in a single government department in the history of our republic. They included: Steve Ailes, Robert Anthony, Colonel George Brown, Harold Brown, William Bundy, Joseph Califano, John Connally, Alain Enthoven, John Foster, Eugene Fubini, Roswell Gilpatric, William Gorham, Morton Halperin, Charles Hitch, Paul Ignatius, William Kaufmann, Tom Morris, Russell Murray, David McGiffert, John McNaughton, Paul Nitze, Colonel Robert Pursley, Stan Resor, Harry Rowen, Jack Ruina, Cyrus Vance, Paul Warnke, Adam Yarmolinsky, Herb York, and Eugene Zuckert.

They, along with my key military advisors—in particular Generals Maxwell Taylor, Earle G. Wheeler, and Lyman L. Lemnitzer—tutored me in all aspects of security affairs: the translation of foreign policy into military strategy, the development of force structure from strategy, the application of military power in pursuit of political ends, and so forth.

The early 1960s offered an unusual opportunity to reappraise U.S. and NATO nuclear strategy. William Bundy, Enthoven, Hitch, Kaufmann, McNaughton, Nitze, Rowen—along with Jerome Wiesner, McGeorge Bundy, and Carl Kaysen in the White House —contributed to the gradual evolution of my thinking on this subject. From those beginnings have come many of the ideas expressed in this book.

Academicians working at the Brookings Institution, Harvard, MIT, Cornell, and Stanford—including Graham Allison, Albert Carnesale, Paul Doty, Sidney Drell, Richard Garwin, Kurt Gottfried, Joseph Nye, George Rathjens, and John Steinbruner—through stimulating debate, and at times harsh criticism, have often forced me to reexamine my premises.

More recently, my thoughts have been influenced by my work with McGeorge Bundy, George Kennan, and Gerard Smith on two articles we published together in *Foreign Affairs* (Spring 1982 and Winter 1984), and by my discussions with Professors Hans Bethe and Kurt Gottfried leading to an article published by Dr. Bethe and me in the *Atlantic Monthly* in July 1985. This book includes excerpts from the *Atlantic* article and from one I had published earlier in the Fall 1983 issue of *Foreign Affairs*.

Spurgeon Keeny, Eugene Fubini, Adam Yarmolinsky, Jack Maddux, and Vice Admiral John M. Lee reviewed parts of the manuscript and offered perceptive comments. Madalene O'Donnell and David Halperin served as extraordinarily diligent and scholarly research assistants. And Jeanne Moore, my never-complaining secretary, worked nights and weekends through innumerable drafts and changes to produce the final text.

I am enormously grateful to them all.

Index

ABM Treaty: *see* Antiballistic
Missile Treaty
Abrahamson, Lieutenant General
James, 91, 96, 101, 102,
108, 129, 160–61
accidental-launch problem, 110
action-reaction phenomenon,
52–55, 59
Antiballistic Missile Treaty and,
55–58
ADMs: *see* atomic demolition
munitions
air defense systems, 31, 42
Air Force, U.S., 44, 51
Alsop, Stewart, 46
Andropov, Yuri, 50–51
Antiballistic Missile (ABM) Treaty
(1972)
development of, 55–58
Soviet violations, 68, 128
Strategic Defense Initiative and,
108, 129
strengthening of, proposed,
128–30
U.S. violations, 128–29
antisatellite weapons
ban on, proposed, 129–30
Soviet advantage in, 61–62
as Strategic Defense Initiative
countermeasure, 161–63

arms control
compliance issues, 69–71
long-term objectives for, 62,
127–32
missed opportunities, 62–67
nonaligned and neutral nations,
role of, 143
nuclear buildup, effects on,
73–74
nuclear parity and, 45
offensive-arms control, 109, 130
political reconciliation, relation
to, 85–86
"proportionate responses" policy
(U.S.), 71
risks of, 63
Soviet advantages through,
alleged, 72–73
Soviet sincerity re, 130–32
Soviet violations, 67–68, 69, 128
Strategic Defense Initiative and,
105–7, 127–28
technology, role of, 144
trust and, 68
U.S. violations, 70, 128–29
verification systems, 68
see also Antiballistic Missile
Treaty; elimination of
nuclear weapons; SALT I;
SALT II